AF182375

Into all the Parish

INTO ALL THE PARISH

Pioneering practices for every local church

Greg Bakker and
Tina Hodgett

CHURCH HOUSE PUBLISHING

Church House Publishing
Church House
Great Smith Street
London SW1P 3AZ

ISBN: 978-1-78140-476-8

Published 2026 by Church House Publishing

Copyright © Greg Bakker and Tina Hodgett 2026

All rights reserved. No part of this publication may be reproduced or stored or transmitted by any means or in any form, electronic or mechanical, including photocopying, recording, or any information storage and retrieval system, without written permission, which should be sought from: copyright@churchofengland.org

The authors have asserted their right under the Copyright, Designs and Patents Act, 1988, to be identified as the authors of this Work.

The opinions expressed in this book are those of the authors and do not necessarily reflect the official policy of the General Synod or The Archbishops' Council of the Church of England.

Scripture quotations are from the New Revised Standard Version of the Bible, Anglicized Edition, copyright © 1989, 1995 by the Division of Christian Education of the National Council of the Churches of Christ in the USA. Used by permission. All rights reserved worldwide.

The Scripture quotation marked (MSG) is taken from The Message. Copyright 1993, 1994, 1995, 1996, 2000, 2001, 2002. Used by permission of NavPress Publishing Group.

EU GPSR Authorized Representative
LOGOS EUROPE, 9 rue Nicolas Poussin, 17000,
LA ROCHELLE, France
E-mail: Contact@logoseurope.eu

No part of this book may be used or reproduced in any manner for the purpose of training artificial intelligence technologies or systems.

Contents

Introduction

Who is this book for?

This book is written for those who are deeply committed to the Anglican parish church and believe it has a critical role to play today in the spiritual life of the nation.

As we write, we have in mind people who want to lead congregations through a process of culture change and who are looking for tried and tested parish-based tools and skills to do this in a way that starts where people are and tries not to leave anyone behind; this is a way that honours the history of the existing members of the congregation with their parish church, as well as the time, prayer, money and effort they have invested in its life and future.

In the pages that follow, we offer proven routes towards creating a healthier balance in church life between who we are and what we do together, putting an emphasis on the kind of presence we hold in a community. We share ways of enabling whole congregations to become more fully alive as individuals, to participate more fully in processes of discernment and decision-making, and collectively to become even more the Christlike people God is calling us to be.

We are writing for churches who take seriously their responsibility for the cure of souls across the whole parish and seek to extend it in practical, visible ways towards a wider range of people – beyond those who will naturally turn to the local church for Sunday services and occasional offices.

If you're willing to take a few risks, try a few new practices and tools, fail and then try something else, then this book is for you. In other words, it is for you if you're willing to step off the path with Jesus and find the new adventure into which he is calling your parish church, benefice or deanery.

Pioneering vs parish?

The purpose of this volume is to enable all parishes to organize their common life around the priority of fostering conditions for newness that will flourish under the guidance of the Holy Spirit, while at the same time honouring and sustaining all that is valuable and healthy in the existing tradition of the church.

For some readers, the combination of 'pioneering' and 'parish' might raise eyebrows, as these concepts have often been set against each other. 'Pioneering', as we understand it in this context, indicates:

- the desire of the congregation to be caught up in the flow of the Holy Spirit;
- a congregation moving outwards to where people are unconnected to the life of the church;
- a willingness to accept the challenge of uncertainty and adventure;
- a turn towards improvisation and adaptability, where strategic planning leaves room for new things to emerge.

A parish that is willing to explore pioneering practices accepts that new things are possible – unexpected new things

– as a congregation steps out in faith, following the breadcrumb trail of the Holy Spirit. The role of the priest and PCC in this way of being church is critical. It is a challenging role of holding space and advocating for what is emerging while affirming and sustaining what is time-honoured and enduring. This role might be compared to that of a parent who is introducing a new baby into a family of older siblings. The new baby's arrival requires a readjustment of the attention and resources in the family so that all learn how to flourish together in an evolving reconfiguration of relationships and reallocation of time, space, attention and finance (among other things).

What can pioneering practices help to achieve?

The aim of adopting pioneering practices is to reach a wider range of unconnected people. A priest receiving a licence from the bishop is invited to 'receive the cure of souls which is both yours and mine', and a parish that welcomes pioneering practices aims to make this cure of souls as real as possible to everyone in the parish. Each parish priest holds responsibility for enabling those who are unconnected with Christianity to draw closer to Christ. In many situations now, this is only possible if the church goes to where these people are because – according to research from the early 2000s – they are highly unlikely to come to us.[1]

1 Tearfund, 'Churchgoing in the UK', *Tearfund*, April 2007, http://news.bbc.co.uk/1/shared/bsp/hi/pdfs/03_04_07_tearfundchurch.pdf, accessed 2.1.2026.

While recent trends have shown younger adults actively searching out churches and becoming more open to faith, parishes nevertheless have a gospel mandate in post-Christian Britain to go where unconnected people are, redirecting the attention, resources and activity of the congregation – particularly towards those at the edges.

It has been said we are living in a time similar to the earliest days of the church. In this book we record examples of where we have seen the Spirit of God act in ways reminiscent of the Acts of the Apostles in, for example: renewing some of the long-held traditions and practices of the faith community; partnering with some of the most unexpected individuals and communities to bring about change; taking unpredictable and indirect routes to a desired destination; reimagining ways of being together with God in community; and fostering unity in diversity.

Training in pioneering practices

The authors of this book are the co-founders of a small training organization called Pioneering Parishes, which started in the Covid lockdown of May 2020. Much of what we offer here is the result of our learning from serving as priests in time-honoured parish churches in different parts of England, and from priests and resourceful lay people we have met in the course of training. Greg's experience is based on 30 years of serving as a parish priest in a variety of contexts. He has served as training incumbent for five curates, most of whom had pioneering gifts. Tina, after a period of senior leadership in secondary education, served in pioneer roles as curate and team vicar in churches where resourcefulness and imagination were required to lead traditional congregations to make connections with people in the local community. We first met while serving as pioneer enablers in diocesan roles. In the early days of the Covid-19 pandemic we brought our shared belief and experience that the parish church is a natural home for pioneering to begin a series of webinars on this theme when online learning became common.

We and the training we offer are categorically and unapologetically for the parish church: for the continuation of a Christian presence in every place, and an honouring of the faithfulness of generations of worshippers in towns and villages across the country.

Starting from where you are

We have been training parish clergy, and engaging lay people, deaneries and diocesan support staff in lockdown, and in person, for almost five years. On a recent residential training weekend, one sceptical curate publicly expressed her fear that we were offering 'yet another initiative' requiring additional energy and resources. She wanted to resist a mindset she felt was foreign to the Anglican tradition and that was a denial of the value of what was precious and beloved in the parish church. By the end of our time together she agreed this is not what the Pioneering Parishes training is about; since then, she has given generously of her time to advocate for our work in her networks and contributed to our recent independent research project, whose encouraging outcomes are summarized as follows:

> *Pioneering Parishes' gift to the church is not in offering any kind of prescribed strategy for mission or growth, but*

in helping a parish reimagine its identity and purpose such that mission and growth are made possible again.[2]

To this end, we start with an appreciative enquiry into what is good, and invite congregations on a journey of discovery with God that members can help shape as they participate in discernment and decision-making. It's an approach that starts where parishes and people are and focuses on helping them to see things differently, discern together where God is at work, use what resources they already have (perhaps in a different way), and be courageous in stepping out in faith.

The postures, practices, tools and skills we offer have been worked out mainly by Greg, always with the aim of enabling a parish church to realize its call to lay down its life so that others might have the opportunity to know the love of God for them.

Both of us have invited congregations to get out of the boat of 'business as usual' for the sake of connecting with those beyond the walls of church. We have worked relationally with cautious congregation members and potential community partners to grow new things on small budgets that reveal something of the kingdom of God, and create possibility for developing faith and discipleship both in the cradle Christian and those who have no experience of Christianity.

We are inspired by a God who honours the potential of the small beginning.

2 Pioneering Parishes Research Report, https://churchmissionsociety.org/wp-content/uploads/2025/11/Pioneering-Parishes-Research-Exec-Summary.pdf, accessed 2.12.2025.

What this book is not

We do not offer a programme. The book does not offer a quick fix to prevailing conditions in struggling parish churches or offer a recipe for speedy growth. It is not an off-the-peg, step-by-step, linear route to a stated goal.

Instead, we offer an invitation into a way of being. For the parish priest it involves wearing a particular set of lenses on parish life, and being able to see the culture of the parish with clear sight, appreciating whatever is good and, where necessary, having the courage and skill to challenge and change that culture to be more in keeping with the life and teachings of Jesus.

Our aims rest on the assumption that the role of the parish priest and PCC is to set the conditions in which growth is possible, and to leave the timing, nature and direction of that growth to God. It is our desire to help congregations let go of the natural instinct to try to control outcomes to preconceived ends, and in doing so help people to grow in personal faith and discipleship and be surprised by what God creates in their midst.

Pioneering postures and practices

The postures of a parish wishing to be radically open to new connections and possibilities in this way are:

- A sustained practice of discerning the presence, voice and activity of the Holy Spirit.
- A clear shared, agreed identity and purpose.
- A stable foundation for making decisions together.

- An acceptance of disruption of the status quo.
- A willingness to give oneself away for others.
- An openness to the goodness of God in individuals and communities beyond the walls of church.
- A willingness to try, fail, lament, take risks and allow God to do some pruning.
- A belief in God's ability to provide the resources for the work he is calling us to do.
- A commitment to different expressions of church that coexist in a community of churches.

Establishing these practices and postures in an established church can be challenging and will require skill, persistence, courage and long-term commitment and vision. Over time we have summarized them into a list of five key dynamics and created a visual interactive tool – a 'roadmap' – that can be found on our website. The purpose of the roadmap tool is to help a parish evaluate its progress towards demonstrating the key dynamics in its shared life, and determine how it can move forward on the journey towards becoming more open, innovative and in tune with God's Spirit, while holding fast to the best of its tradition.

The key dynamics of pioneering

We have chosen to structure the chapters of this book around the five key dynamics. They are:

1 Congregational spiritual discernment: the transformative skill of noticing.
2 Agreed missional values: the power of principle over preference.

3 Shifting your heart, attention and resources outwards: losing your life to find it.
4 Trusting in God's abundance: what do you have in your hand?
5 Different ways of being and doing church: equal, connected and distinct.

In the ensuing chapters we will try to outline these clearly so that you will be able to act on the dynamics yourselves in your own context. We trust you can do this and, with the help of God, you will.

We have shared the writing of the book between us. Greg has written Chapters 1, 2 and 5. Tina has written the Introduction, Chapters 3 and 4, and the Conclusion.

As you read on ...

We hope this book makes you dance for joy as it affirms your own instincts, pioneering practices, and your part in the movement of the Spirit that is guiding many parish priests and PCCs today.

If, on the other hand, it makes you feel uncomfortable at times, we invite you to try to sit with any emotions it awakens and see where they take you. That too is part of pioneering practice.

We hope that by embarking on the steps offered here you will discover that the God you serve is stranger, more wonderful and more committed to your ongoing transformation – and that of your congregation and wider community – than you could have imagined.

1

Congregational Spiritual Discernment: The Transformative Skill of Noticing

We use tools for congregational spiritual discernment in order to shape the future in the flow of God's Spirit

We aim to discern together what the Holy Spirit is inviting us to be and do by being present to the 'now': we pay attention to and try to notice what is going on in our congregations, in our local community and in our inner selves. We adopt practices of spiritual discernment to help transform congregations into active participants in whatever is emerging through the work of the Spirit around us. We expect God to guide us not only through Scripture and church tradition but also through contemporary culture and the created world.

An older couple as a model of congregational spiritual discernment

Congregational spiritual discernment is a foundational practice that marks the entire journey of a pioneering parish church (or pioneering deanery). At the very heart of this dynamic is a growing awareness and conviction that God has more for us as communities of faith.

God's invitation to Abram and Sarai (Abraham and Sarah) is a story that pioneering parishes tell themselves frequently while on this journey:

> *Now the LORD said to Abram, 'Go from your country and your kindred and your father's house to the land that I will show you. I will make of you a great nation, and I will bless you, and make your name great, so that you will be a blessing.' (Genesis 12.1–2)*

Here we glimpse something of God's desire to bless the world. This yearning to bless, to our unexpected surprise, involves human participation. God's chosen approach to engaging the world is not a 'do to' method. Rather, God inhabits a 'do with' relational model. God's intention is to work through an older couple, Abram and Sarai, whose names are later changed to Abraham and Sarah.

As the story unfolds, we discover that God's invitation involves a profound unsettling of the very comfort structures they have erected for themselves. This particular couple are older. Abram, we are told, is 75 years old. They are embedded deeply in family and home. There are indications that they have accumulated much wealth (Genesis 12.4–5). Into the security of what Abram and Sarai know, God essentially says: 'I've more for you than this. I have something I want to show you. But you can't see it from where you're standing. Will you come with me on a journey of faith and discovery?'

Abraham and Sarah, of course, were not perfect people. In fact, the Bible doesn't gloss the scenes where we glimpse them at their worst as people. Sadly, both activate horrible plans along the way that diminish others and themselves.

Nevertheless, God is committed to engaging the world through them. God's very nature leads God to work relationally with and through people. This 'do with' approach to engagement leads to the birth of a clan, even though both Abraham and Sarah's bodies were considered 'as good as dead' (Romans 4.19; Hebrews 11.12). God's 'do with' ethos unfolds over many generations, culminating in the birth of Jesus, 'son of Abraham', who would unlock 'grace upon grace' for the world (Matthew 1.1; John 1.16). And through faith in Jesus, all who believe in him are celebrated as Abraham and Sarah's 'children' and inherit the invitation to play a part in God's blessing of the world (Galatians 3.7–8).

The outworking of the Christian journey is linked with the story of God's commitment to an older couple who lived thousands of years ago. Like Abraham and Sarah, church congregations are invited into an ongoing rediscovery that God does indeed have more for us as communities of faith. Whether we are younger or older, there is a human desire to be part of something that matters, something that raises the low bar of aspirations into life-giving adventures with the God of Jesus, who this very day is calling church communities to set aside comfort and security in order to discover what we can't see from where we are standing.

Abraham and Sarah's willingness to journey with God, to believe that God had something more for them, is a foundational narrative of all churches walking the pioneering parishes' path.

For congregational reflection

- *To what extent are we as a congregation inspired by Abraham and Sarah's story?*
- *In what ways is God's relational 'do with' approach to engagement surprising and challenging to us as a congregation?*
- *To what extent are we as a Christian community of faith stepping outside of what we are comfortable with so that we can notice together what the Spirit wants to show us?*
- *What evidence is there to support these responses?*

What is congregational spiritual discernment?

The congregational spiritual discernment that Pioneering Parishes envisions is not a programme demanding all kinds of additional activities and expenditure. Yes, of course, the practice of congregational spiritual discernment can be challenging and require adjustment. What is being suggested is more about our disposition, a way of being present to God, our communities and ourselves as congregations.

Like the experience of Abraham and Sarah, congregational spiritual discernment is daring to believe that God has more for us, and making the journey to discover what this is. Congregational spiritual discernment is about cultivating a disposition of noticing what God's Spirit is showing us. God is inviting us to dismantle the siloed way we often think about church, home, work, play and the world around us. In all of these things, the Spirit of God is in the flow of activity; and what is asked of us is to be present to the 'now' and to pay attention to what we see unfolding in our midst.

Noticing as a disposition of being engaged doesn't just happen, however. Often, our capacity to pay attention to the present moment is nurtured through simple spiritual practices or tools that we, as Christians, already have in our toolkit. Frequently, congregational spiritual discernment can be practised by adapting the focus of what we are already doing.

Tools for congregational spiritual discernment

This section offers four tools. Some of these tools can be cultivated more easily than others. These offerings recognize that there is sometimes a level of growing into the use of these tools.

The Examen

For 11 years, I was the Vicar of St Mary's, Sholing, a parish church in urban Southampton. The congregation enjoyed being together and they loved worshipping as a faith community. They were activists and committed to demonstrating God's love to the wider community. Rather than launching all kinds of additional activity, my colleagues and I decided that a modified form of the Jesuit Examen would be taught and incorporated into acts of worship and meetings. The aim was to use what was already happening to encourage the practice of noticing and celebrating where the congregation saw signs of love, life and goodness in the wider community.

The form of Examen we used at St Mary's incorporated these questions:

- Where have you noticed God's grace, love, life and goodness this week?
- Where did you recognize that you got in the way of God's grace?
- To whom can you be a blessing this coming week?

At the start of each service (which were mostly eucharistic), the congregation rehearsed what they had noticed during a short section called 'community time'. The second and third questions were incorporated into the confession and the prayers.

What happened was that the members of our congregations became more expectant that God would reveal something. The congregations knew they would be asked the question each week about what they had noticed. The Examen helped cultivate within our congregations the practice of noticing life, love and goodness at work in our homes, relationships, community activities, and creation itself.

One of the most exciting discoveries came through Sandra, who was a member of the congregation and a lollipop lady at the local primary school across the street from the parish church. Sandra noticed that no matter the weather, mums and carers often stood outside of the gates talking with one another at the end of the morning school run. Sandra shared her noticing and wondered if the church might be able to support the community spirit that was already present. With prayer and conversation with the school, a group of school-aged mums hatched a plan and 'Refuel' was born. Each Friday morning during term time, the church hall was opened, good coffee was provided and toast was served. The space was full of laughter and good conversation. 'Refuellers' shared their lives with one another. Connection, authenticity and support were hallmarks of the gathering. Organizationally, Refuel was a huge deal for the church congregation – low volunteer time was required but there was high relational impact.

From this simple act of hospitality each week, St Mary's was able to connect with a whole range of people who became actively supportive of the church's mission in the community. What we discovered was that many in the Refuel community, most of whom would never come to a Sunday service, shared the outward-looking values of St Mary's and were prepared to do things to make ministry happen. And in their participation, other opportunities opened for the parish church to nurture their exploration of Christian faith.

For congregational reflection

- *Many Christians have a personal practice of noticing things for which they are grateful. How might our congregation build on personal devotional practice and develop this into a shared communal practice of spiritual discernment? (Keep it simple!)*

The 'balcony view' of noticing

I learned to be an incumbent in a small village of 80 residents. In this parish, the PCC included almost all the members of the congregation. Every other month, 14 PCC members squashed into the tiny village hall. As a new incumbent, it was my first ever meeting in the chair of a PCC meeting. I opened with a prayer and then the meeting was 'off': the room was full of passion, diverse opinions, much talking over one another and muttering to neighbours. After about 20 minutes, I stopped everything and asked the PCC members:

'Is this how you always behave?' There was a stunned silence as the PCC allowed the question to hang in the air.

Over time, the quality of our meetings significantly improved. There was still passion and diverse opinion, yet they grew in their capacity to listen intently, laugh with joy and recognize what God was doing in their community. Five years later, as I was preparing to leave the parish, one of the PCC members commented: 'The best thing you ever did for us was ask us that question, Is this how you always behave?'

What this story showed me was that church leadership is not about getting one's way. Rather, shared leadership involves noticing and inviting others to step back and be aware of what is happening. Often, the naming of what is unfolding helps others to see more clearly.

In business theory this type of leadership is likened to the ascending of stairs to the balcony overlooking a dance floor – hence the term 'balcony view'. Often our congregations are immersed in the immediate and urgent matters as well as the clash of personal preferences as to how an issue should be resolved. Without the view from the balcony, parish churches and leaders are frequently reactive in decision-making.

The practice of moving to the balcony view opens the opportunity for congregational spiritual discernment. This practice helps leaders to recognize that every PCC conversation has the potential of being an act of congregational spiritual discernment.

Spending time on the balcony is also vital for glimpsing the big picture of how the congregation is doing. For some leaders, ascending to the balcony is found through work with a coach who asks good questions that invite 'big picture' noticing. One rural vicar I know with five parishes attributed the fruitfulness of his ministry and congregations to regular engagement with a coach. He remarked that the coach helped him to step back from the activity and glimpse a larger perspective, which unlocked a renewed sense of purpose and direction.

For PCCs, this practice can be expressed by allowing ample time in meetings for honest conversation about mission, and how the congregations are doing in the practice of their aspirational values and vision.

For congregational reflection

- *What might the impact of our PCC meetings be if several participants were intentionally given the role of figuratively standing 'on the balcony' and doing the work of noticing?*
- *What is the expectation in our congregation that our clergy practise the 'balcony view' of noticing? What might have to be adjusted in parish life for this practice to be developed and celebrated?*

'Dwelling in the Word'

It is a challenge that exists in every group of people. Whether it is in a meeting or a group discussion about the meaning of Scripture, the same people – generally clergy and men – fill much of the space in terms of sharing their thoughts. While there might be wisdom shared in these regular contributions, other insights and observations are also likely not to be heard in such an environment.

In Pioneering Parishes training, a go-to resource for noticing is called 'Dwelling in the Word'. This unique approach to listening for God through the noticing of others was developed as part of the Partnership for Missional Church project, which was for a time housed within the Church Mission Society.

Congregational spiritual discernment involves creating space for all to be included in conversations about the life and mission of the church. Often, the control of biblical interpretation is in the hands of 'the powerful' within a group, whose training in a particular interpretative way translates into a sense of responsibility for bringing everyone to an 'orthodoxy' of belief. (Be not deceived – this happens in all theological traditions of the church!)

The Dwelling in the Word process is aimed at cultivating an environment where each participant is seen, heard and valued. Dwelling in the Word is a way of proceeding rooted in humility towards other participants and God's Spirit. Humility in this instance means that the aim of the exercise is to listen and understand, not to correct or challenge the interpretation/contributions of others even if we might disagree. From insights shared, the process moves into a noticing of what the Spirit is saying within a given group gathering.

Dwelling in the Word is, in many ways, like the practice of *Lectio Divina*. In congregational settings, *Lectio Divina*-type practices are often avoided out of the fear that someone will say something 'heretical' or odd. This is a legitimate concern. But when fear gives way to the need for control, the only voices that will be heard are the 'authorized' or 'powerful'.

The Dwelling in the Word process follows these steps:

1. We invite the Holy Spirit in prayer to open our ears, hearts and minds.
2. We listen to a passage of Scripture read out loud and notice where our attention is drawn – a verse, phrase or a single word?
3. We then remain in silence for a minute or two, staying with the place in the passage that stood out for us.
4. We each find a person in the group whom we might call 'a reasonably friendly-looking stranger'.
5. We listen to that person as he or she says what they 'heard' in the passage in a particular verse, phrase or even single word. They may mention something they'd never heard before, something odd or something comforting, or something about which they'd like to ask a Bible scholar.
6. Listen well, because your job will be to report to the rest of the group – in fours, sixes or the whole group – what your partner has said, not what you yourself said. Some people even take notes to help them focus and remember. You introduce your partner by name to the group and share what you heard them say. Each person takes their turn when they are ready to speak.
7. If there is time, a conversation develops around what God is saying to us today from the themes arising in the whole group.

As a priest who uses communal spiritual tools like Dwelling in the Word within Sunday acts of worship, I have found that there is often a broader depth of collective insight accessed beyond what can be said by the single voice of the preacher. And almost always, what was an 'odd comment' or even a 'theologically incorrect' one just faded away. Only twice have I ever had to say: 'I am not understanding what you're trying to communicate. Where might I find that in the text/story?' Mostly, what was not helpful or meant for the congregation dropped away as we noticed the beauty, insight and wisdom being unlocked by the Spirit of God through this practice of congregational spiritual discernment.

For congregational reflection

- *To what extent are we as a congregation practising openness in a way that cultivates space for all to be seen, heard and valued?*

The Five Marks of Mission

The Five Marks of Mission is a theological framework for seeing and discovering what God is doing in the world. The Five Marks set out a holistic description of God's committed engagement with our world through human involvement. The formulation of the Five Marks began in the mid-1980s and was subsequently adopted in 1996 by the General Synod of the Church of England.

One of the striking features of the Five Marks is the 'both/and' vision that cuts across the theological polarization of previous generations by holding together the essential work of proclamation and transformative social engagement. While these Marks are still not universally accepted within the Church of England, this framework for seeing is rooted in God's 'do with' ethos of engagement with the world:

1 To proclaim the good news of the kingdom.
2 To teach, baptize and nurture new believers.
3 To respond to human need by loving service.
4 To seek to transform unjust structures of society, challenge violence of every kind, and to pursue peace and reconciliation.
5 To strive to safeguard the integrity of creation and sustain and renew the life of the earth.

Within this theological framework, no Mark has priority over the others. Rather, each Mark is intended to be recognized as equal, connected and distinct; and a unique expression of God's activity through human involvement. This approach is analogous to Paul's teaching on the body of Christ in 1 Corinthians 12 and Romans 12. There are many parts, but one body. Each part has a role within the greater whole.

On occasion in our Pioneering Parishes training, we encounter a different narrative at the grassroots level. Sometimes when we describe various pioneer projects to engage with unconnected people, the first question usually asked is about proclamation and nurture. There is a strong concern at the grassroots level that the church's mission is not simply 'social work'.

What we are describing here is indeed more than social work. At the same time, within the Five Marks framework, 'social engagement', as well as creation care and the human need, is a good in itself.

The trajectory of a pioneering parish is to cultivate spaces alongside established congregations for unconnected people to encounter a life-transforming encounter with Jesus. Frequently, there is significant relational work to be done prior to the forming of new Christian communities or fresh expressions of church. Nurturing authentic relationships and goodwill within local communities takes place prior to proclamation and discipleship. We would also affirm that pioneering activity that does not include proclamation and discipleship is missing some of the essential dynamics of mission.

I wonder how often congregations do *notice* – but are not really doing the work of spiritual discernment. I wonder if – when we start with proclamation – it is easier to fall into a 'do to' approach to mission: we have the answer you need; we know what you need; we're not authentically interested in you as a person beyond your noticed need for Jesus.

I remember some years ago saying in a clergy gathering that many people were not going to engage with us until we were willing to acknowledge the good within them. The push-back from this comment was enormous. Yet my comment is profoundly rooted in a robust doctrine of creation, which affirms the grace of God's goodness flowing and unlocking beauty in all that exists. A dynamic perspective such as this recognizes that grace builds on what is already good. Indeed, such an understanding reveals that the very nature of Jesus' gospel is to draw forth the good in all living things.

Applied to humans and local communities, spiritual discernment means looking intently for the evidence that God's image within us has not been obliterated (tarnished yes; destroyed no). Noticing such goodness and beauty shifts our perspective and even enables us to confront gracefully the darkness of those things that draw us away from God's 'do with' communal approach.

I wonder if the present ordering of the Five Marks limits our ability to notice. What if the apparent prioritization of proclamation conditions our perspective to focus on a narrow definition of 'spiritual' with its emphasis on personal sin and salvation?

These wonderings are in no way a repudiation of the need for tending to that which diminishes life (that is, sin). But God's mission is larger than a message that gives priority to an interpretative methodology of noticing focused on the sinfulness of the people standing before us. What if, in this season of church history, we reordered and practised the Five Marks in a contextually appropriate way?

1 To strive to safeguard the integrity of creation and sustain and renew the life of the earth.
2 To respond to human need through loving service.
3 To seek to transform unjust structures of society, challenge violence of every kind and pursue peace and reconciliation.
4 To proclaim the good news of the kingdom.
5 To teach, baptize and nurture new believers.

What would we notice if our seeing and practice were transformed? What if, for the sake of love, we joined with those of goodwill in what God is doing in our local communities? What would we notice if we approached such activity as a good in itself, worthy of doing simply because we affirm love, life and beauty? What would people of good will notice if followers of Jesus lived in this way?

Having proposed the significance of the practice of congregational spiritual discernment in a pioneering parish, we move to offer an approach for establishing firm foundations for congregational life, relationships and decision-making.

For congregational reflection

- *To what extent do you feel that the church's capacity to notice the breadth of God's engagement in the world is hindered by making proclamation the most important Mark of Mission?*

2

Agreed Missional Values: The Power of Principle over Preference

We base our decisions on agreed missional principles rather than individual preferences

We agreed missional principles (values) with our congregations(s) and engaged members of our wider community and made these the basis for our aspirations and church decision-making; we have written descriptions of what our life together looks like, sounds like and feels like when our agreed values are shaping our behaviour; we have embedded values into our church structures, systems and practices. The PCC regularly reviews our progress towards living out our values as part of its ongoing work.

Agreed missional principles as a foundation for congregational life

Many years ago, my parents moved on to a new housing estate in California. The houses were beautiful and the gardens were immaculate. It was the kind of place where neighbours expected one another to maintain their homes and front gardens to a high standard. Well, the neighbours were quickly disappointed when my father got to work on his front garden.

The first thing he did was return the space to that of a building site – he immediately took out the turf, flowers and trees that the contractors had planted! For months, my father dug out the soil by hand and removed all the builders' rubble, which had been buried instead of being taken away. The hostility of the neighbours intensified when he had several loads of steer manure dumped in the garden. In the hot California climate, the smell was nauseating. Nevertheless, my father persevered until he was satisfied that the soil would nurture fruitfulness. Only then did he replant the turf, flowers and trees. What became apparent shortly afterwards was that all the neighbours' gardens began to wither and die. In the end, my father took on sage-like status in the neighbourhood and enjoyed many years of talking with neighbours about their gardening issues.

My siblings and I have retold this story many times at key points in our lives. My father taught us that there are no short-cuts to cultivating fruitfulness in life. Frequently, it means slowing down and doing the significant work of cultivating a soil that can host beauty and life.

This, I have discovered, applies to parish churches. Cultivating the soil of church culture – the way things are done – is foundational to the unlocking of life, energy and love. And in pioneering parishes, the way the culture of a congregation is shaped flows from the intentional discernment and practising of shared agreed principles (values).

Why do we need agreed missional principles in our congregations?

There are two reasons why we need shared agreed principles in our congregations. First, agreed principles raise aspiration.

Church communities today often face the strong pull of two powerful dynamics. The first gravitational pull is towards panic. Many leaders and congregations are increasingly worried about the future. Will there be a Christian presence in every part of this land within a few years? To whom shall we pass on our cherished church? There is an urgency for change, with many congregations being warned repeatedly that they will die without it. A sense of panic can motivate action, but it frequently results in poor decision-making and the dishonouring of relationships.

I was trained in an Anglican theological college where the maxim 'maintenance is failure' shaped our perspective and submerged into the very depths of the unconscious mind. We were sent to all kinds of seminars and workshops on how to grow churches beyond 200 members. When I hit parochial life in the Church of England, I instinctively saw the barriers to congregational development (and numerical growth). And in those early years, I felt driven, frustrated by the slow pace of change and the disappointment of why I wasn't fulfilling the outcomes of what my training told me should happen if you did certain things. It led to a place of deep panic and not being more discerning about the pace of change adapted. Thankfully, I worked with a gentle and kind churchwarden and a wise wife who both challenged me about the way my training blinded me from seeing the realities of the context more clearly and the impact that my disappointment was having on those around me.

Frequently, panic within congregations can be expressed in a 'try harder' mentality. This mindset can stoke all kinds of activity and the expenditure of resources. The trap, however, is that this can occur without pausing to discern together what is happening and what adjustments to mind-set and practice might be required. Panic also strengthens within us the mindset that restoring our fortunes is down to us or a 'saviour' leader saving the day. Sadly, this is a recipe for bruised and broken relationships as well as exhausted clergy.

There is another gravitational pull in play within parish churches: the tug towards the comfort of the familiar. In the face of much bleakness and scarcity, some congregations decide repeatedly to stick with what they like and know. Sometimes this is expressed explicitly. Some years ago, a congregation in the United States declared boldly in its parish profile/advertisement that they wanted a priest who would not meddle with change, and was happy to stick exclusively to the work of chaplaincy and pastoral care.

My experience has taught me that dwelling in the comfort of the familiar potentially exposes us to the virus of judgementalism. Sometimes those who are happy with the way things are start to blame and shame 'those people out there' who don't want to participate in our activities and services. They ask: 'What's wrong with these people?'

While rare, there are those in congregations who say publicly that they don't care whether the church community dies, as long as they have what they already have until they are gone. (Yes, I have heard individuals in several different parishes say this. These particular individuals, who sometimes see themselves as the shapers of opinion, have often been able to block spiritual and congregational development for decades.)

Generally, the decision not to change is much more subtle. It can be expressed in the desire to welcome others, while expecting newcomers to conform, to like things done the way that the existing church community does things. Such a mindset is really a decision to dwell in the comfort of familiar ways.

Neither powerful dynamic is capable of nurturing aspiration within the human heart. It is what happens between the extremes of panic and the familiar that is significant. The Pioneering Parishes approach is persuaded that genuine aspiration flowing from the Spirit is raised in contexts where both panic and comfort are set aside.

What does setting aside panic and the comfort of the familiar look like? Let's be honest. It is entirely true that there is a bleak future without renewal within our parish churches. But neither is there any guarantee that change will stem the tide of scarcity and decline.

However, there are questions, when faced honestly before God, that can ground us against the extremes of panic and the familiar. These key questions for exploration are rooted in a sense of aspiration around congregational identity and vocation. Two questions pioneering parishes frequently ask are:

1. What kind of people do we aspire to be together for God and our local communities?
2. To what extent are we prepared to journey with God into the unfamiliar, trusting that we are not alone as we walk together, and that God has something to show us that we are unable to see from where we are currently standing? What evidence is there for our conclusion?

The raising of aspiration around congregational identity and vocation within the mission of God is life-transforming. Aspiration is key to a life-giving release from panic and the pursuit of the comfortable and familiar within a parish church. Agreed missional values then become the verbal and embodied expression of a congregation's aspirations. And for those parish churches who walk the journey of vocational aspiration with God, it subverts Christian discipleship as a programme and converts it into a transformational, participatory process of congregational change with deeper insights into who we are in God and our unique contribution to the work of God in a beloved world.

The second reason for agreeing shared principles is that it offers greater clarity for congregational decision-making.

In Pioneering Parishes training sessions, participants sometimes tell us that shared agreed principles (values) are unnecessary. 'We have the Bible. We have Jesus. What more is required?'

What we in the Church of England generally fail to appreciate is that it is easy for both clergy and congregations to fall into the trap of being governed by preference. This is often revealed in the way church communities communicate and make decisions.

For example, an upset parishioner once complained to me at the conclusion of the service: 'You played the wrong tune.'

I asked kindly: 'Do you mean that you prefer another tune? Or do you think that particular tune is somehow objectionable?'

The parishioner replied: 'Oh, the first; I like a different tune.' Then she smiled with the realization of what she had said.

When I introduced a regular use of the *Lectio Divina* – a 1,500-year-old Christian spiritual practice – into the Sunday Eucharist, I was met with these types of comments:

> 'It just doesn't feel right.'
> 'It is not proper; it doesn't look Anglican.'
> 'We don't do things like that here.'

All of the above are subjective statements of preference.

Of course, we need to take seriously the feeling that something is not right. Sometimes it does not feel right because it is *not* OK. But sometimes 'It just doesn't feel right' can also mean 'I'm uncomfortable because I'm being invited into the unfamiliar and new.'

The notion that there is a proper way of doing this is equally subjective. The concept of 'properness' is an imaginary, even in the Anglican tradition. When we speak about church, each person is operating from a picture of what church should look like. And in helping congregation members to unpick the comment 'We don't do things like that here', what they meant was that in our parish church we don't want discussions within the service where the perspectives of lay people are welcomed.

There is nothing wrong with preference. As human beings, we are hardwired for diversity. We all have likes and dislikes. We all have preferences about how something should or should not be done. Diversity is one of the great delights – and challenges – of being human.

The question that pioneering parishes ask, however, is this: 'Should preference be the basis for decision-making in the parish?' Tina and I are persuaded that a dynamic mark of a pioneering congregation is that decisions are based on agreed missional principles (values) rather than individual or congregational preferences.

For congregational reflection

- *What does the language of preference sound like in our church community? Give examples that have been heard in your congregation.*
- *How might agreeing missional principles enhance our congregational life?*

Agreed missional values as conversation

In pioneering parishes, shared agreed values have the feel of a conversation about what matters to us in terms of our aspirations and identity as participants in God's mission to a beloved world.

Developing shared agreed values is a conversational process. Pioneering Parishes offers specific training about how to organize and facilitate a values-based discernment conversation. In this section, we'll reflect on the conversational nature of agreeing missional values.

First, agreeing missional values as a process includes existing congregations, but is not entirely an internal conversation or exercise.

Existing congregations have a key part to play in the agreeing of values. Often, those who have been connected for some time can give insight into what is valued about the church ('What do you love about this church?') and how these values can help build for the future ('What do you want this church to be known for in the wider community?').

The challenge is that the views of long-standing members are not the only perspective available to us. It is well established within Benedictine monasticism that not all voices carry the same weight. Surprisingly, there is an assertion in the Rule of Benedict that God often gives the necessary insight to move forward to the newest members of the monastery (church community). Benedict recognized that newer members frequently see things in a way that most long-standing members cannot. And so, in the conversation, the responses of newer members – say, under two years – are in some way given greater weight. (In one parish I served, each conversational response from those who had been members for less than two years was weighted 1.5; the weight of responses from long-standing members was 1.0.) The goal in the conversation is not to determine majority opinion, but to listen carefully for the whisper of the Spirit (often spoken by the newer members, according to 1,500+ years of Christian tradition).

In addition, people of goodwill – residents, schools, businesses and charities – in the wider community have a contribution to make to the church's conversation about values.

The wider community has a part to play. A clergy colleague once told me that 'non-Christians' and people who didn't attend services had nothing to say to the church about God's mission in the world. Yet my experience teaches me that some people who don't attend public worship have a keen interest in the presence and ministry of the church in a particular place. Sometimes these voices might seem to us rather 'traditional' and 'outdated'. And yet there are people in our local communities who are insightful, hopeful about the presence of the church and willing to help when included.

Of course, it is simply not possible in most instances to include everyone in the wider community in such conversations. We, however, must seek ways to invite people of goodwill with whom we already have some connection/working relationship into the conversation about church values.

Lastly, our agreed values must include a mechanism for change/newness. Jesus' gospel is all about change and transformation. Pioneering congregations have agreed principles that intentionally cultivate space for change/newness. It is entirely possible to adopt values that provide no *mechanism* for congregational change, but at least one value needs to specifically make room for change to be openly explored.

At St Mary's in Sholing, where I was vicar, the primary value was: 'We will be an innovative environment.' Evidence statements were added to describe what was meant by 'innovation'.

In my work with Holy Trinity Church in Fareham, the words 'change' and 'innovation' were disliked. Instead, the congregation and PCC chose the word 'humility', and developed evidence statements as a suitable lever to explore and embrace the need for a change of attitudes and practice within the church community.

Take adequate time to consider the language you will use to communicate the necessity of ongoing change.

For congregational reflection

- *The process of discerning values is relational in nature. There are many ways to invite congregations and people of goodwill into conversation. What will work best in our context?*
- *Where have we seen instances in which God has helped the church move forward through the suggestion/idea of a newer member or someone with a loose connection to the congregation?*

The necessity of evidence statements to illuminate values

Many congregations have spent time coming up with a list of values. What we frequently realize in our training is that once agreed missional principles have been identified, the work appears to stop in many parishes. What we find is that congregations can agree a list of up to six words or short phrases, but still have a lack of clarity around the meaning of the values. The significant work comes in describing meaning.

For instance, many churches have something like 'love people' as a value. It is a superb value; it is one that Jesus gave his followers. The challenge within a congregation is that we assume the meaning of 'love people' is self-evident or that we all have a shared understanding of what Jesus meant. And frequently, what happens is that a chaotic low bar on understanding and behaviour dominates. But if we gave explicit descriptions, as Jesus did, of what 'loving people' looks, sounds and feels like in practice, we might raise vocational aspiration within the congregation.

What we have found is that most people struggle to intuitively make the connection between a statement of principle and expected behaviour. This isn't because of a lack of intelligence. This is down to the way the brain is wired in most people. Consequently, evidence statements help a wider range of people to make the connections between the agreed principle and what it might look, sound and feel like when something is being put into practice and when it is not.

Earlier this year, Pioneering Parishes was invited to offer training for ordinands. The training was hosted in a school. In particular, our training was done in a mathematics classroom. To our great delight, we noticed the maths teacher had developed agreed principles with her students *and* evidence statements to accompany the values.

The posted agreement in this classroom was that students owned responsibility for their learning. What owning responsibility meant was then illuminated in practical statements:

- We use the resources available to us – brain, books, board, asking a buddy before asking the teacher.
- Be brave and think for yourself.
- Have your own views.
- Think about alternative solutions.

Notice the specificity of what owning responsibility means in this classroom. The function of evidence statements is to describe what will be seen, heard and felt in the environment when the values are being lived out.

Evidence statements that work well also include a description of what will be seen, heard and felt in the environment when the values are not being lived out.

In one of my parish churches, the congregations had an agreed missional value to be intentionally engaged with the local community. Based on the teaching of Jesus, who said, 'Let us go on to the neighbouring towns, so that I may proclaim the message there also; for that is what I came out to do' (Mark 1.38), the congregation adopted evidence statements to help identify when this value was not being put into practice. For example, the evidence we'd expect to recognize when we were not being intentionally engaged:

- If we are not developing new relationships outside the church community, or if our 'relationships' are superficial or affected.
- If we are too busy talking – or just too busy – to really hear what other people are saying.
- If we are not attempting to discover what people in the local neighbourhood need, or if we believe – or simply assume – that we already know without asking.
- If we make decisions based only on our own needs or the assumed needs of our neighbourhood.
- If we express an inward-looking bias towards those within our church community.
- If we automatically dismiss new and uncomfortable ideas or those that require us to take a risk.

Notice again that the examples are specific and thoughtfully move beyond the superficial. These evidence statements for this value called the congregations to greater maturity in understanding and behaviour as Christian communities of faith. And when the evidence statements are prayerfully constructed, agreed missional values are transformed from being generic bland words into the Spirit's tool for raising aspiration and deepening communal spiritual development.

For congregational reflection

- *Imagine you are observing a classroom where being curious is a stated value. What do you expect to notice within this environment? What does 'curiosity' look like? What does it sound like? What does it feel like?*
- *If our congregation has a statement of values already, do we have evidence statements that illuminate meaning? If not, explore together the meaning of the value and write statements that help to identify when values are being put into practice and when they are not.*

The impact of making decisions based on agreed missional principles

What might happen when principle becomes the basis for decision-making in the parish church?

In my experience at Sholing, there were five significant developments. First, the role of the PCC was transformed, although it took time for it to adapt. But instead of being involved in the nitty gritty about whether to put a new type of loo roll in the toilet facilities, the PCC took primary responsibility for assessing how well we were living out our values. By the time I left the parish, the PCC was generally using the first portion of its meetings to reflect on how we were – and were not – putting our values into practice.

In addition, in decision-making situations, members of the PCC quickly learned to bring the evidence statements into the discussions as a way of reminding us what kind of people we wanted to be for God and for our local community. The agreed values and evidence statements transformed members of the PCC into active participants in spiritual discernment about our identity, aspirations and ministry.

Further, our values also shaped our preaching and teaching. We spent almost six months preaching about the values in all our Sunday services. Our values, we believed, were gospel values. So we used the lectionary to illustrate these values. There was an expectation for all staff members – both lay and ordained – that we would apply our values explicitly in our preaching and teaching week by week. We even incorporated this expectation into our sermon/teaching feedback forms.

Moreover, the agreed values became a basis for reflecting on all ministry in church, whether lay or ordained. As an incumbent, I was committed to putting into practice the values the congregation had agreed. Similarly, the expectation was that all paid staff, clergy colleagues, licensed lay ministers and partners (volunteers) shared this commitment. PCC members were elected on the basis of their willingness to make decisions based on the shared values. Our conversations about aspiration, behaviour and the exercise of ministry were rooted in our agreed missional values, which we saw as a reflection of Jesus' life and teaching. Certainly there were differences of opinion, but the values provided a firm foundation for robust, constructive discussions within the church community, within the PCC, and for reflecting on the exercise of ministry by volunteers within the congregation.

Lastly, the agreed values changed the tone of our conversations within the congregation.

When people complained that the noise in Sunday services had increased, the values-based response was: 'The congregation told us that they wanted us to be a diverse multi-generational family.'

When 'non-religious' events in the church raised objections, the values-based reply was: 'The congregation affirmed that they wanted our buildings to be used more widely by the local community.'

We kept the response factual, rooted in *what had been agreed* with the congregation's involvement.

The pivotal moment for me as a leader came when a parishioner verbally attacked me because she wasn't getting her way: 'You're not listening to me!' I replied calmly: 'I am listening to you; I simply disagree.' The agreed values gave me the confidence to articulate this.

One of the greatest joys for me was the day I had a breakthrough conversation with someone who didn't like what was happening in the parish. Previously, our conversations had been guided largely by personal preference. On this occasion, this valued member of the congregation made a critique of something taking place on the basis of our agreed values. We didn't agree, but our reflections together on the issue were robust and transforming.

I learned how important it is for leaders to reply factually rather than emotionally. I learned how significant it is to acknowledge feelings of preference without judgement. Generally, preference will offer a glimpse of personal needs or reveal a spot where someone is stuck in their Christian journey, and this can change the whole tone of a conversation. I'll say more about how this transformation happens in Chapter 5.

I am immensely proud of the many parishioners who have struggled with the participative change process in the congregations I've led over the years, but who have stuck it out. It still bewilders me how in the midst of much disruption, even newcomers have been prepared to help shape a different way of being a parish church. And for me, the greatest joy as a pastor is to recognize within congregations a deeper sense of aliveness as we've journeyed together. The discerning and practising of shared agreed values has been the best congregational discipleship programme I've ever participated in – and facilitated – because it created the conditions that allowed churches to shift their hearts, attention and resources outwards towards those who were unconnected. This is the theme of the next chapter.

For congregational reflection

- *What is our response to the impact of making decisions based on agreed missional principles?*
- *To what extent are the impacts described in the section above currently reflected in our congregation and PCC?*

3

Shifting Your Heart, Attention and Resources Outwards: Losing Your Life to Find It

We shift our heart, attention and resources towards people who are unconnected

We listen to those who are on the fringes of our church congregations and respond to their views and aspirations for the church. We find out what they think and need, rather than tell them what we want them to hear. We find out what will be attractive to them and hold lightly to those things we have learned to love; we shift our resources towards those who are as yet unconnected to God in Christ.

The owl story

It was a regular PCC meeting. Dull, you might say. Covering the usual bases. Until the question came up: a wedding couple had requested that their rings be delivered at the appropriate point in the service by owl. Would the PCC give their permission?

The meeting erupted on all sides with energy, emotion and opinion. All the pros, cons, preferences and possibilities were aired, with the responsibilities of the PCC and the prerogatives of the congregation mainly in mind, until the chairperson asked: 'In whose interests are we making this decision?' and the animated voices fell silent, brought up short. It was a powerful question, and it made everyone think.

Who is the church for?

'In whose interests are we making this decision?' is a good question for any PCC, and it's linked to another fundamental one: 'Who is the church for?' Archbishop William Temple is attributed with a pithy answer: 'The church is the only organization that is run for the benefit of its non-members.' Dietrich Bonhoeffer put it in a more radical way: 'The church is only the church when it is the church for others.'

Stepping back to take a 'balcony view' over the New Testament we see how the movement towards others, outsiders – non-members if you will – is evident in the life of Jesus and the Acts of the Apostles. The pattern and goal of a life under the direction of the Holy Spirit is one that moves outwards from the believing community towards the life and communities beyond it.

In the Gospels we see how God in Jesus 'became flesh and blood, and moved into the neighborhood' (John 1.14, MSG). The Son of God lives among, pays attention to and listens to his fellow humans and thus learns about our ways of being and doing. Once Jesus' ministry begins, he allows his attention to be diverted by what is happening around him, by the needs, questions and challenges of others. He tells his disciples they must be willing to lay down their lives if they want to be his followers, and models what this looks like by being prepared to step out of a fruitful, rewarding life at a relatively young age, for the sake of people he does not know and an outcome that is not guaranteed.

I have worshipped and served in a number of churches that appeared to be healthy or even had a reputation for being missional. All of them welcomed new people and hoped they would be included in the existing congregations and offer their gifts and service to the worshipping life of the church. I am not sure many would have said they believed the church existed for the benefit of people who weren't present. I wonder if some congregation members consequently missed out on the adventure and transformative experience of going to where others were and discovering God at work in ways they had not previously considered.

For congregational reflection

- *What requests have been made of our church or PCC that caused lively debate? What principles form the basis of decision-making in this kind of situation?*
- *To what extent would we say we are a church 'for others'? What is the evidence for this evaluation?*

Each congregation is an expression of the body of Christ

In Pioneering Parishes training sessions, I like to play with the metaphor of the body of Christ. I find it useful to imagine the congregation as an individual person – as a single disciple – one expression of the body of Christ. It helps to get away for a while from thinking about the church organizationally, and to look at familiar situations through different lenses. It also reshapes us to think more collectively, as the monastic orders did, about congregational life lived together for a shared purpose.

Once a church has begun to be shaped around a set of values, as we described in Chapter 3, it will begin to present itself to the outside world as an organization with a discernible and dependable character. For example, if the congregation chooses to have values of openness, compassion and creativity, people who encounter the church will, over time (by God's grace), consistently be met with these characteristics as though the congregation were an open, compassionate and creative individual. The church might even become known as an open, compassionate and creative presence in the community, just as an individual Christian might.

An open, compassionate and creative church would be a valid – if limited – expression of the nature of Christ. Such a congregation could collectively embody, represent and enact in its life together the character, postures and practices of Jesus in relationship to its wider community and context.

What would it look like if a congregation embodied the life of Jesus in its community?

At Pioneering Parishes we suggest that a congregation embodying the life of Jesus will go to where people are, allow the church's attention to be diverted and its direction rerouted by those beyond its walls, and be willing to lay down its life for the sake of its community.

Individual Christians often do these things as part of their personal discipleship; however, here the focus is on the whole congregation acting out their discipleship collectively, and intentionally shifting the church's heart, attention and resources outwards. Towards the end of this chapter we offer a tool for discerning how to do this wisely, listening to all perspectives while keeping firmly in mind the question: 'In whose interests are we making this decision?'

Going to where people are

It is possible to go to where unconnected people are literally, or emotionally, psychologically and spiritually. Even in a small parish there are places where people gather: schools, pubs, parks, playing fields, clubs. In my first parish on an outer urban housing estate there were very few meeting points, and people gathered mainly at bus stops, so we used our imaginations to find ways (resourcefully but not very successfully) of engaging with them there (chocolate and Advent calendars played a role!).

Going to where people are can simply involve building authentic relationships in the natural course of things, listening to what matters to people, finding out what they care about and discerning if there's something the church can do about that, perhaps in partnership with others in the community.

It can also mean choosing to allow them to have their wedding rings delivered by owl.

Allowing others to divert our attention

In parish life we can be so focused on our own plans, struggles and preoccupations that we do not notice what is going on around us when there is something important God is gently inviting us to pay attention to through the voices or activities of those who are outside our organization.

In their book *Being Interrupted*, Al Barrett and Ruth Harley describe various stories from the Gospels in which Jesus allowed himself to be interrupted, diverted from his purpose and drawn in a different direction by something that happened unexpectedly. In Mark's Gospel the 'interrupters' are listed as the Syro-Phoenician woman, the woman with the haemorrhage, the woman with the alabaster jar, and the children the disciples tried to shoo away from Jesus.[1]

If people beyond the walls of the church believe we are open, compassionate and creative, they may invite us to get involved in community events and enterprises. (These are not the only values that would encourage people outside the church to engage with us of course; they are just three examples.)

In some congregations, invitations from community organizations to join in with them and help may create issues of capacity; we want to be available and supportive but volunteers may already be giving their time to keeping the 'church show on the road'. In situations like this the tool we introduce towards the end of the chapter can be useful in determining how we wisely distribute our available resources in a fruitful way.

1 Al Barrett and Ruth Harley, 2020, *Being Interrupted: Reimagining the Church's Mission from the Outside*, London: SCM Press, pp. 89–114.

For congregational reflection

- *Are we in our parishes prepared to be interrupted and diverted from our current practices by people who don't belong to our congregations?*
- *To what extent do we as a congregation go to where people are?*

Laying down our life

In the lectionary for Lent, congregations are reminded that on the way to the cross Jesus says: 'For those who want to save their life will lose it, and those who lose their life for my sake will find it' (Matthew 16.25). Most hearers will interpret this as an individual encouragement to lay down their own personal aspirations, desires and plans and offer them to God to use in his service and the service our neighbours. However, if we continue to think of the congregation as a single expression of the body of Christ, and remember that Jesus laid down his life so that he might 'draw all people to [himself]' (John 12.32), we could inhabit this advice collectively as a church.

The act of dying to self is a turning away from our own ego, from a desire to put our own needs and wants first, to keep ourselves safe and happy and to secure our future. In Pioneering Parishes we are convinced that the role of the congregation is to give itself away for the sake of the local community: not recklessly, but as the Holy Spirit leads each individual church through communal spiritual discernment, trusting God for its future. In doing so we find our life again, individually and collectively, as our faith is stretched and our discipleship worked out more fully in encounters with others beyond the walls of church.

In one of Greg's churches, the imperative for self-giving was expressed as part of a value of generosity. An evidence statement stated that the church had a 'generous bias' towards those who were unconnected to its life. This provision allowed for an appropriate amount of time, attention and resources to be spent on sustaining and developing the ministry of the church for those who were already present. At the same time, it ensured that the centrifugal pull of the existing church's needs didn't overcome the imperative to move outwards to others in the community for whom the incumbent also had a responsibility for the cure of souls.

To do this in the current climate of anxiety requires courageous faith from the church leadership. It seems counter-intuitive at a time when volunteers, generosity and money are often in short supply. But we are convinced God can be trusted to bring life out of death.

To finish the owl story: the PCC had a productive debate about the wedding couple's request to allow owls to deliver the rings. Their eventual decision to say 'Yes' was provisional on a small number of conditions aimed at ensuring the safety of all concerned as well as good stewardship of the building. It reflected a willingness to go to where the couple were, be diverted from business as usual, and lay down the church's natural instinct to do what was apparently in its own best interests for the sake of others. It demonstrated a generous bias towards people who were not part of the regular worshipping community.

The decision-making spectrum

In Pioneering Parishes, in these kinds of cases we use a tool called the 'decision-making spectrum' (Figure 1). It consists of a simple line with arrowheads at each end; one end is marked 'Those already present', while the opposite end marks 'Those who are unconnected'.

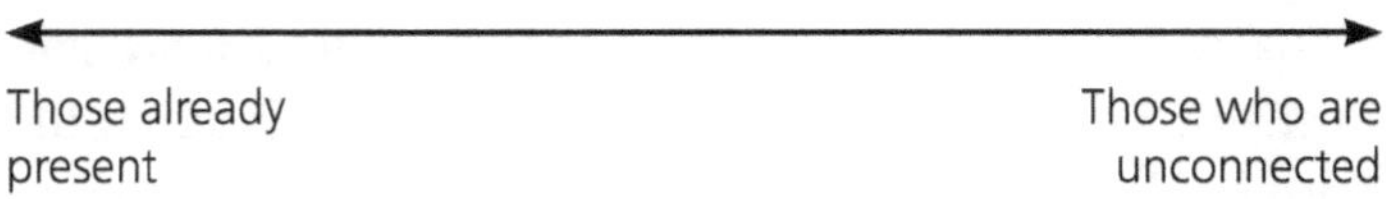

Figure 1: The decision-making spectrum

The spectrum can be useful in conversations at PCC meetings or in other decision-making spaces to help decision-makers think through the question: 'In whose interests are we making this decision?' Participants can be invited to place themselves somewhere along the spectrum in a position that represents their own response to the question of whose interests they believe a decision should serve. This can be done by physically moving in the room or by indicating a point on a line on a page. Each person can be invited to explain what considerations or context have caused them to stand in that place, making for a rich discussion.

It is a tool that brings unspoken attitudes and assumptions into the open and allows honest debate without judgement. Once all views have been aired, people can be invited to move again if they wish before a final decision is agreed. This can create a strong visual confirmation of where consensus lies. Sometimes the decisions are legitimately made in favour of the existing worshipping congregation, and at other times these may be set aside for the sake of others.

In Pioneering Parishes we have learned a great deal from an experienced leader of a Benedictine convent community, Sister Joan Chittister, who asks not only: 'Who benefits from this decision?' but also: 'Who profits from it remaining unchanged?'

The second question is useful in making participants in the decision-making process more aware that no outcomes are neutral. Retaining the status quo is a decision that will favour some over others.

A question of capacity

Perhaps the thought of having to engage with those who are unconnected to church fills you and others in your church with a sense of overwhelm. Shifting your heart, attention and resources outwards feels like another demand on shrinking resources when there is little capacity even for the things that have to be done: putting together a PCC, keeping accurate accounts, managing safeguarding well, ensuring Sunday services happen.

We will raise the question of creating capacity at greater length in the next chapter, but for the moment we concentrate on sharing a process for enabling the church congregation or PCC to discern collectively if it has the capacity to undertake or continue to offer a particular activity, service or event that involves going towards people beyond the worshipping congregation with the possibility of building new relationships.

Sargeant's non-profit matrix

We use a tool called 'Sargeant's non-profit matrix' (or matrix map) employed in the non-profit sector and adapted for a church context to assess the attractiveness of a particular activity, service or event against the congregation's capacity to run it. This tool enables a not-for-profit organization with a small amount of funds to allocate its resources to fulfil its missional purpose to maximum effect.

The matrix is composed of a table of nine squares:

External attractiveness: How attractive would this be to those who are unconnected to the church?

1	2	3
4	5	6
7	8	9

How much capacity do we have to do this?

Figure 2: Sargeant's non-profit matrix[2]

Sargeant's matrix invites leaders to view church activities, services and events: first through the lens of attractiveness to

2 Based on Adrian Sargeant, 2009, *Marketing Management for Non-profit Organizations*, 3rd edn, Oxford: Oxford University Press, Figure 3.5, 'Nonprofit Portfolio Analysis'; Figure 3.6, 'Using the Portfolio Model', pp. 91, 93.

people on the outside; and second, through that of congregational capacity.

Congregations or PCC members are invited to determine where on the matrix they would place the activity under discussion. Guided by their particular perspective, individuals place the activity or plan in different rectangles, explaining the basis of their decision. Some might feel there isn't enough capacity, others feel there is. Some have reason to think it will be highly attractive, others doubt it. Similarly to the decision-making spectrum (Figure 1), this tool facilitates honest and open conversations in which everyone can participate on an equal footing. Such conversations have the extra benefit of increasing participation in, and ownership of, the community life of the church.

The criteria for assessing external attractiveness

The assessment of external attractiveness considers:

1 The potential of a ministry/project to attract, as pioneering parishes are focused on the unconnected with whom they want to engage and serve.
2 The extent that something will be positively supported and participated in by people in the wider community.
3 The capacity to attract external volunteers and funding unconnected to the church.
4 The extent to which something furthers the values and outcomes that the congregation aspires to embody. In this case, the aim is for the wider community to recognize that the parish church is good news for the community.

The criteria for assessing internal capacity

The second assessment is the capacity for the church to deliver plans/projects/activities to a high standard. It asks crucial questions like:

1. To what extent do we have the energy and space required to offer the activity/project to a good standard?
2. To what extent are our teaching/training/groups helping church members grow in confidence as followers of Jesus?
3. To what extent do we have the contacts/volunteers with the skills necessary to undertake the proposed activity?
4. How much will the activity/project cost and to what extent are financial resources available for the expenditure?

In Figure 3 below we show how box 1 is the place for activities the church believes will be attractive to those who are unconnected to it, for which there is enough capacity. Other boxes represent different judgements.

The matrix is a visual way to help people think through a decision. The idea is to identify where on the grid of nine coordinates you would place a particular project, plan or activity using the two detailed assessment criteria. Placing an activity in most of the coordinates in the matrix (boxes 2–8) indicates that the congregation needs to evaluate the capacity and attractiveness questions carefully before it makes any decision about stopping or reimagining an activity or starting something new; in other words, the church may need to identify and address some of the factors requiring attention before it proceeds. Two examples of this kind of process follow below.

External attractiveness: How attractive would this be to those who are unconnected to the church?

1 High attractiveness; high capacity	2	3 High attractiveness; low capacity
4	5 Moderate attractiveness/ capacity	6
7 Low attractiveness; high capacity	8	9 Low attractiveness; low capacity

How much capacity do we have to do this?

Figure 3: The matrix showing levels of capacity in relation to levels of attractiveness

Reimagining: a craft fair

For example, a church ran a three-day arts and crafts fair annually, attracting people on the fringes of church and raising money for church funds. When, one year, this event was assessed for its viability by the PCC using the matrix, the women who had run the fair for a number of years placed it in box 8. Reluctantly, but with a degree of relief, they admitted that they felt they no longer had the energy to put the fair on, and they felt it was running out of steam.

Such an admission allowed a conversation to take place about what to do. After some discussion and negotiation, a new leader was found, the length of the fair was shortened to a single day, and regular stallholders were invited to bring their creativity to the task of organizing it. As a result, the women who had painfully but honestly acknowledged that the running of the fair was becoming a burden to them were able to lay it down with dignity. In addition, because the new leader was able to engage a different group of people as stallholders, volunteers and punters from the margins, the volunteer base of the church widened. A wonderful side benefit was that it raised more money in that one day than it had in previous years in three.

Creating capacity for something deeply attractive

During his time in Southampton, Greg's church was considering a project that addressed child school holiday hunger within the community. He shares in the following paragraphs how a well-established grip on the principles of Sargeant's matrix already embedded in the PCC's mode of operation played a significant enabling role in helping the church to undertake the project, shifting the congregation's energy outwards.

The church's starting assessment revealed there were deep concerns about our internal capacity to deliver the project. The capacity coordinate would be somewhere on the far right side of the grid, in boxes 3, 6 or 9. We didn't know whether we could recruit enough volunteers. We knew we couldn't operate with 'just enough' crew. We had to have two sufficient levels of reserve volunteers for each role. Another factor was that we didn't know whether we'd have enough money to run the project. Some on the PCC quite rightly said that we couldn't start and then walk away as other 'do-gooder' charities had in the past.

Our initial assumption was that the service would be moderately attractive on the external scale. The coordinate would be in the middle row, boxes 4–6. We knew from the statistics and the local schools that there was a school holiday hunger problem for children. Our question was whether we could actually get families to access the project. For potential participants, there could be a level of shame that would put them off participation. We were also aware from running a foodbank that there was some disgust and resistance in the wider community to 'charity', which transgressed strongly held assumptions around poverty.

So with the issues out on the table aided by the matrix, the next step was to address the factors that might help the church move to a coordinate from which it could proceed with the school holiday hunger club with confidence.

Exploring possibilities

We talked with the schools about how we might overcome the shame factor. They suggested that the invitations come from them and that we use school buildings. This was a huge disappointment to us. We wanted the project on church premises, as this would give us access to new sources of funding to revamp our hall. However, we had to let this aspiration go; and instead we used school facilities for the project.

We engaged local businesses and asked if there were ways they might participate. We spoke to the school catering company. The company agreed to pay the lunchtime supervisors out of their budget to do the cooking. Other lunchtime supervisors wanted to volunteer, and so they did. A local business charity simply wrote a cheque for £2,000 for start-up costs – no questions. There was much goodwill.

The parish church also had to adapt its activities and ideas on a regular basis in order to redirect internal energy. We tried as much as possible to keep the church diary clear in the run-up to school holidays. Staff members and volunteers negotiated availability with one another and families during school holiday time. We figured out where we were able to duplicate as much as possible – especially with craft activities.

External attractiveness: How attractive would this be to those who are unconnected to the church?

1	2	3
4 School holiday hunger club *after* matrix conversation and adjustments	5	6
7	8 Holiday hunger club *before* matrix conversation	9

How much capacity do we have to do this?

Figure 4: Matrix showing the before and after coordinates for the school holiday hunger club debate

Eventually the PCC agreed there was enough potential for the club to be viable, although there was still no guarantee it would work and be sustainable (see Figure 4). Faith was required at this stage – trust that God would provide what was still lacking. The decision was made to go ahead, and it was launched. Everything that was essential was provided, the school holiday hunger club was very well received in the community, and we took it on the chin when people complained about us doing something that had not been done for them when they were younger!

For congregational reflection

- *Choose an activity that is part of church life and evaluate it according to the matrix. Does this event or activity enable vibrant faith in church members and/or draw those who are unconnected to something that is deeply attractive? If not, how could we respond?*

Enabling creative and wise use of resources

Do you categorically need a matrix? No. But churches do need a means to be able to regularly review the activities, services and events they run as openly and impartially as possible, particularly in times when resources are less readily available. The matrix is a tool that helps congregations to see how much energy, time, money and volunteers are tied up in projects, activities and events, some of which may not bear much fruit, opening up the possibility of conversations about wise and imaginative redistribution of resources with a more missional focus. As such, it is like an implement that enables artful pruning, so the church vine can become more resilient and more fruitful in service of its neighbours.

The matrix takes its place alongside the tools we described in Chapter 1 as an aid to congregational spiritual discernment. It encourages a clear-sighted evaluation of the costs of serving the local community. It enables the participation of all in an equal forum and fosters realism about what is possible and what might be ripe for change.

In the next chapter we move on to consider further means of creating additional capacity for events and activities that are attractive to those in the community.

4

Trusting in God's Abundance: What Do You Have in Your Hand?

We cultivate a range of different ways of being and doing church within one parish

We recognize when we are thinking and acting as though God cannot provide for his people or make the resources available to fulfil his call. We believe that God can surprise us with unexpected ways forward and unlock surprising resources. We ask 'What do we have in our hand?', nurture alternative thinkers and encourage new ideas. We are open to seeing things differently. We engage in a cyclical process of evaluating the tradition for what should be retained, reimagining tradition(s), stopping things that are no longer serving us, and starting new things.

We ended the previous chapter describing a process for redirecting resources outwards, for reimagining our activities and refocusing our energies as a parish in the hope of connecting with a wider range of people. We start this chapter asserting the importance of being able to stop running events, activities and services that have come to the end of their natural life in order to release fresh potential. A pair of tools are offered that enable congregations to do this well.

Sargeant's matrix (Figure 2) can play a role here, in giving organizers and volunteers opportunities to admit that it is time to lay down something that has been the object of love, time and care. A couple of days ago I had a conversation with two faithful leaders of a church toddler group that had run for many years. As they told me it had just closed, their sadness was evident, as was their acknowledgement that all the indicators had showed it was no longer serving its original purpose. I have since heard that the parish had marked this faithful contribution to its mission through a well-attended service of celebration as it came to a natural ending.

In our Pioneering Parishes training we make participants aware of how imperative it is for parishes to grieve when some element of church life comes to an end or undergoes significant change. Just as people who lose loved ones or experience other significant losses have to make space to grieve before they can pick up their lives again – having integrated the loss and found hope for the future – so do parish churches.

Grieving for change

In the Psalmic tradition the act of grieving is known as lament, and it is a practice the current church is in the process of rediscovering. It is one that might be more widely embraced given the range and depth of losses that parishioners may be currently undergoing in many areas of their life, including their church. In our training we give a presentation on the spiritual practice of lament, which aids letting go – as well as allowing the expression of anger at injustice and God's apparent deafness to our cries. In this we draw on the work of the cultural anthropologist and Roman Catholic priest Gerald Arbuckle in his book *Grieving for Change*. Arbuckle and the Old Testament scholar Walter Brueggemann advocate equally strongly for churches recapturing the practice of lament, with Brueggemann stating categorically: 'Only grief permits newness.'[1]

We sometimes ask our training course participants what they miss in church life. Depending on the church, this might be a worship band or organist, children in the Sunday service, clergy who do home visits, Harvest Festivals with churches full of fresh fruit, vegetables and specially crafted loaves, the King James version of the Lord's Prayer … this list goes on. The loss of these is a cause of grief for many congregations and Arbuckle suggests that parish priests and licensed lay ministers do not sufficiently recognize the need to facilitate acts of lament for what is passing or has already gone.

Acts of lament

An act of lament can be simple or complex, long or short, but when it honours the experiences of parishioners and meets them where they are, it brings healing. It is this healing that makes way for newness, reducing resistance to change and paving the way to a different future. We have had the privilege in our training sessions to hear some excellent ideas for contextual acts of lament.

One parish priest who wanted to replace an outdated service booklet told us she asked parishioners to mark the words in sections of the existing familiar order of service that

1 Walter Brueggemann, 1986, *The Hopeful Imagination: Prophetic Voices in Exile*, Philadelphia, PA: Fortress Press, p. 9; Gerald A. Arbuckle, 1991, *Grieving for Change: A Spirituality for Refounding Gospel Communities*, London: Geoffrey Chapman.

particularly resonated with them before she invited them all to lay the booklets to be replaced on the altar, and receive a new version of the order of service that had been agreed. Another priest told us he held an act of lament in the church building with silence and candles; attendees entered through one door and left through another, symbolizing a journey through liminal space towards a new beginning. We didn't know what loss the occasion marked, but it seemed simple and profound and he thought it had been effective. Priests and worship leaders can devise contextual acts of lament as necessary for congregational use in all kinds of situations. Regular parishioners too can be invited to write their own individual acts of lament for losses in their personal lives based on templates from the Psalms, which follow a discernible pattern of moving from praise through lament to request to trusting faith.

For congregational reflection

- *What losses do we think we or our congregation might be mourning?*
- *How have we practised lament?*

Encouraging conversations about creative destruction

Acts of lament can help congregations understand the reality of Ecclesiastes 3: 'For everything there is a season, and a time for every matter under heaven: a time to be born, and a time to die.' Equally, thinking about the life cycles of all living things helps to open up these conversations.

The tool we offer in this chapter is the ecocycle (Figure 5).[2] It presents congregations who have perhaps never thought of the parish church as having a life cycle with the natural order of all living things, including organizations: that they are born, reach maturity with time, go through a process of 'creative destruction' – a loss or transition that feels like dying – and then experience renewal, or a gestation period for something new to be born.

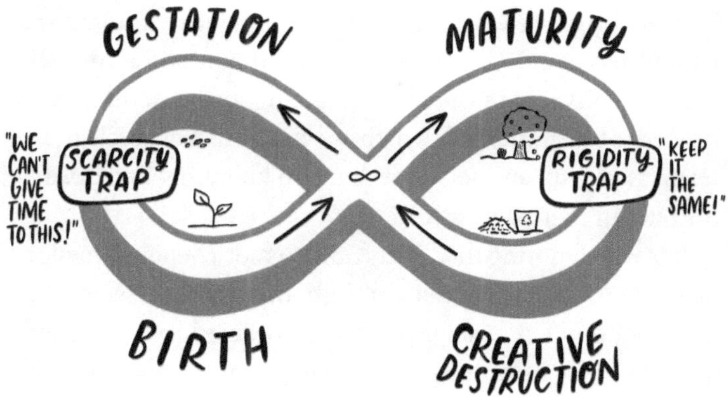

Figure 5: The Ecocycle

It is surprisingly reassuring for congregations to be confronted with this diagram. Like our other tools, it brings unspoken fears and wonderings into the open and allows them to be discussed. It helps congregations understand that endings are not failures, nor even in fact actual endings; it brings relief to understand that in gospel terms, endings or challenging transitions are the gateway to life, birth and resurrection hope.

2 Figure by Sophie Killingsley, based on 'Ecocycle Planning', *Liberating Structure*, https://www.liberatingstructures.com/31-ecocycle-planning/, accessed 4.9.2025.

The 'Rigidity Trap' shown in Figure 5 indicates the point at which those responsible for an activity get stuck in 'business as usual' when it is actually time to lay it down or adapt it to circumstances; creative destruction can be resisted for years in organizations and there is an art to discerning when the right time has come to embrace change. Showing the rigidity trap as a visual fact helps people – the leaders or creators of an activity – to recognize if they are in fact in that trap, and even maybe to laugh kindly at themselves struggling to keep something going when, deep down, they have intuited that its time has come. Choosing to discard or end something that has been of value in the past but is no longer useful is like a process of decluttering, which we know in house-clearance terms is painful and sad but often also liberating and positive for human mental health.

It is worth noting that, according to more detailed versions of the ecocycle, the person initiating or overseeing the creative destruction stage is often considered to be a heretic; he or she may be prophetically challenging accepted ways of being and doing, and is likely to suffer pushback and sometimes even aggressive resistance. It helps to be aware of this in advance.

The 'Scarcity Trap' is the moment when newness can be sensed to be emerging and requires investment to grow. Sometimes it is a question of discerning here which idea of several is the one we will invest in.

This tool can be encouraging for congregations too, as different areas of church activity may be at different points on this loop. While one group of parishioners may be coming to terms with the fact that their area of service is entering a period of creative destruction, another might be celebrating their area of activity reaching a point of maturity, or recognizing that something is starting to bubble up. Overall, the ecocycle helps congregations understand there are seasons in parish life; not just liturgical seasons, but seasons for everything that can be lived with discernment, wisdom and grace.

For congregational reflection

- *How might the ecocycle help us have conversations about endings in our church congregation?*
- *Do we have a process for a regular review of what projects, activities, services and plans might be at maturity, heading towards ending, going through a metamorphosis or coming to birth? If not, what would it look like if we did?*

A scarcity mindset and narrative

It will be clear from the paragraphs above that Pioneering Parishes recognizes that there are reduced numbers and resources across the Church of England at this time. This is objectively true, for example, in reducing clergy numbers and congregations unable to fill PCC places or pay parish share; and there are many other areas where there is a felt absence of something considered necessary or desirable.

This realism is vital. However, when our unrelenting congregational narrative is 'We haven't got enough young families/servers/money/people to manage the accounts', it may be that we have inadvertently fallen into a scarcity mindset, leading to a predominant downward-spiralling narrative about a lack of resources and possibilities. This can manifest in a variety of ways, such as congregations who tell themselves stories about why little can be expected of them or God. Greg recounts how he told one parish where he was the incumbent that they were banned from using the phrase 'We're a poor parish', as it had turned into a mantra, and he could demonstrate all sorts of ways it wasn't true.

The presence of a scarcity narrative is often betrayed in conversation that focuses on what is lacking. Remarks such as 'We're a poor parish', 'We've only got a part-time vicar', 'There's no money for a new boiler', 'We've lost our organist' or 'The church is just a few elderly people' betray a scarcity mindset. It may be true that the parish isn't well-off, the vicar is part-time, there isn't enough money currently to replace the boiler, the organist has left, grown old or died, and the congregation is elderly. These realities may present the church leaders with significant challenges. However, the way the facts are given reveals a particular attitude of mind that emphasizes what is not over what is.

Scarcity mindsets are part of a culture that compares itself – usually unfavourably – with others and with an idealized version of reality. Congregations compare themselves with other churches they know; they also tend to compare the present day with what is probably a rather idealized picture of how things were in the past.

Our ecclesial imaginary

Neuroscience tells us that we hold an 'ecclesial imaginary' – a mental map in our minds of what church looks like, informed by the previous experiences we and others have had, stories we have been told and images we have seen. The imaginary is not necessarily accurate, as our brains have a tendency to oversimplify reality and our memories can be unreliable. An imaginary is a simplified model for ease of use, and whatever it holds – full church buildings, a specific pattern and provision of services, a permanently available parish priest and thriving youth group, according to the impressions we hold from our past – has arisen from human experience. None of these are immutable factors in a flourishing church. It is possible for a fresh imaginary to develop as we explore adaptive ways to respond to the current context.

In the field of mental health and well-being it is well attested that a mindset of gratitude and a regular practice of appreciating the good things in our lives can change our inner disposition and move us towards hope. A pioneering parish is committed to a posture of thankfulness and appreciation of what already has been given (see Chapter 2 in respect of setting values on the basis of the question: 'What do you love about this church?'). In the rest of this chapter we will suggest a number of small ways that, taken together, have the potential to shape a different imaginary for the church, help them adopt a more positive outlook, and create capacity for newness.

For congregational reflection

- *Does our congregation have a scarcity narrative? If so, what does it sound like?*
- *What is our ecclesial imaginary? What is our ideal picture of a flourishing church? Could this change?*

Surprising abundance

We move now from a consideration of scarcity narratives to a narrative of surprising abundance. We note the ways the people of God in Scripture are continually caught out at the point of rehearsing their narrative of scarcity by God's abundant provision; for example, the Exodus stories of manna and water being miraculously provided in the desert, jars of oil and flour that don't run out for Elijah and the widow of Zarephath, the feeding of the 5,000 and 4,000, Peter's miraculous catch of fish.

When one of our earliest course participants, Ali Mascarenhas, started a community gardening enterprise in the parish churchyard that relied on volunteers from the village, the lack of sufficient power tools became a limiting factor in the project. Smaller secondhand tools were donated courtesy of an appeal in the village newsletter; but one day she said to God: 'We don't have enough power tools. What can I do?' The following day she had a phone call from someone she had never met but who had read her request for donated tools in the newsletter. The caller told her to buy the remaining tools she needed and send him the receipt. After checking she was hearing correctly, and that he understood how much the tools would cost, she bought the tools she needed, thankful for his incredible generosity and the grace of God in hearing her prayer and indicating she was on the right path.

Greg and I are convinced that God provides the resources for whatever he calls congregations to do. As team vicar in Portishead, I believed God had called me to invite the whole town to a free lunch for the Diamond Jubilee of Queen Elizabeth II. The full story appears elsewhere,[3] but for the sake of this chapter I can report that all the resources needed to feed thousands were provided via community organizations, the specialized skills of individual congregation members,

3 Tina Hodgett, 2020, 'The Big Free Jubilee Lunch', in Cathy Ross and Humphrey Southern (eds), *Bearing Witness in Hope: Christian Engagement in Challenging Times*, London: SCM Press, pp. 51–6.

the collaboration of ecumenical partners and large numbers of willing volunteers. God even provided me with peaceful sleep through the anxious planning period, and with dry weather on the day when it was raining everywhere else. (Watch the TV footage of the national celebrations on the day of the Queen's Diamond Jubilee for proof that this is true!)

The church where I served was not particularly wealthy and the budget for the event was surprisingly small. But through the extraordinarily generous collaboration of a wide range of churches and community partners, God's surprising provision was released and together we fed and watered 3,500 people for free.

It is noteworthy to me that this kind of abundance is often made available for community projects in a way it may not be for church-based projects. Through this and other ventures over two decades, I have come to realize that what may appear as God failing to provide for church congregations as he did in the past may simply be a gentle invitation to move outwards, try a fresh approach, be adaptive and imaginative, connect with those in the community and see what is possible from there.

Moreover, pioneering parishes recognize that prioritizing real relationships, offering people the opportunity to exercise their individual passions, gifts and skills, opportunities to engage in play, and a desire for a 'story-rich life'[4] can release unexpected capacity and energy in generous measure.

4 Ann Morisy, 2004, *Journeying Out: A New Approach to Christian Mission*, London: Continuum, p. ix.

Celebrating and fostering volunteers

Working with volunteers is one of the great privileges of parish ministry. It can also be frustrating working with those who at any point may withdraw their involvement for personal reasons. We have learned that valuing volunteers highly through thoughtful and conscientious processes of recruitment and affirmation, plus a bit of playfulness, raises the bar and inspires others to join in.

In his low-income, inner-city benefice, Greg held an annual volunteer celebration in the style of an Oscar ceremony. Parishioners relished the opportunity to dress up and play at being celebrities, and new volunteers were rarely hard to find, particularly as the term of their ministry was set clearly from the beginning.

Where it is hard to find volunteers, it may be that God is waiting to call people to different things. Ali Mascarenhas, mentioned earlier, was fulfilling many of the roles required by a faithful member of a small rural parish church. She was on all the rotas and was PCC secretary helping to hold the parish ship steady, but she also had gifts of creative imagination and glass art, as well as a passion for the gospel and the environment, and skills in volunteer management from an earlier career. It is this package of skills, gifts and passions that has allowed her church to play a significant role in the life of the local community. However, had she remained in her role of trying to maintain the status quo, it is unlikely any of the developments that have been fruitful in the life of her church and community would have taken place.

The model of service in parish life suggests that a specific and limited range of gifts is desirable and valuable: accountancy, musicianship, flower arranging, cleaning, gardening, preaching, pastoral care, reading Scripture, leading intercessory prayers ... all of these are good gifts that have served the time-honoured church well. But what if people with different gifts can open up new areas of connection with the community: bike repair, for example, or classic-car restoration; drama or massage therapy; clowning or dance; expert wildlife knowledge, and so on? There are plenty of stories of how these gifts are creating an interface between church and community across the country and the Western world, and allowing faith and church practice to flow in between.

It might be possible in this way to create a different imaginary of what church can be – perhaps you no longer need people to sew hassocks, for example, but the gifts and skills that enabled their creation might have a role to play in a different project that brings church and community together in the future.

Part of the Abraham and Sarah story involved the couple seeing the possibility of a new horizon. Older congregations may tire of fulfilling volunteer roles where they have served for decades, but still be up for a new challenge. I call to mind a 92-year-old in Portishead who relished any opportunity to leave her sheltered accommodation and venture out into the community with God, bringing as her gift an ability to strike up instant friendships with anyone. This led her to a morning of slicing lemons at the local Flower Show (among other similar adventures).

For congregational reflection

- *How do we celebrate volunteers? Do our volunteer recruitment and management processes make people want to be involved and to feel valued?*

- *How might the gifts and skills that congregation and community members have and want to share become facilitators of community connection, or in some other way help embody one or more of the Five Marks of Mission?*

What do you have in your hand?

In a way, looking at the skills that are in the congregation – which may not be those that have traditionally been sought in congregational life – is about looking with fresh eyes at what you have in your hand. 'What do you have in your hand?' is the question God asks Moses in their encounter at the burning bush (Exodus 3—4).

As God calls Moses to confront Pharaoh and demand that Pharaoh lets the Hebrew slaves go, Moses rehearses his narrative of scarcity: 'I can't speak fluently,' he protests. 'I can't stand up to Pharaoh. I can't convince him you sent me. I don't have the authority or leadership skills to lead the Israelites.'

God asks him, 'What do you have in your hand?'

What Moses has in his hand is simply his shepherd's staff. It's just a long pole of wood. He has probably developed such familiarity with it in his life tending a flock of sheep that he hardly notices it's there.

The staff under God's direction becomes an extraordinary and unexpected agent in all the stages of the exodus from Egypt as Moses follows God's call: the means of demonstrating his authority, releasing water, parting the Red Sea, initiating the plagues. While our current situation is not quite as dramatic as a test of strength between YHWH and an Egyptian Pharaoh, in Pioneering Parishes we believe parish churches can expect the same God to open our eyes to familiar people and things in a fresh way and reveal their unexpected God-given potential. Congregational life then shapes itself around what is gifted in the moment rather than according to a past tradition or ideal. I have seen this resourcefulness shape worship gatherings round beach labyrinths, in private gardens, with jazz bands and folk music and in many other forms.

Nurturing a space for new ideas

Pioneering parishes create space for new ideas to be aired, celebrated, improved and, as appropriate, acted upon. This requires particular skill from the chair or facilitator of a group to create the conditions where new ideas are welcomed and not instantly shut down, and where an initial idea can be built upon by contributions from others. I liken the practice of keeping an idea in the air to a game of 'keepy uppy' – when a group of football players tries to keep a football off the ground for as long as possible.

It is tempting for all to see the negative sides of an idea, or to remember when it was tried before with not much success. On the other hand, it takes courage to share an idea with other people, risking critique, so we recommend thanking the idea-giver for being willing to share it: 'Thank you for your idea.' It may be brilliant, feeble or foolhardy, but it allows an opportunity for the chair/facilitator of the group to ask if there are any other ideas and, if so, lead a discussion on the comparative merits of the ideas that are shared. You might want to use a tool such as Edward de Bono's Thinking Hats,[5] which reviews ideas from five different perspectives

5 Edward de Bono, 2009, *Six Thinking Hats*, London: Penguin.

to consider the different ideas, or one in particular, at a later stage. When a front runner has been established, the question 'How can we make this idea even better?' keeps the idea in the air for even longer.

These ideas can be about anything, from how to create a parish profile to how to bridge the gap between the church congregation and those least likely to come near it for fear of shame and rejection.

Dreamers who do

The dreaming space is where people with a specific set of gifts come into their own. Some people are created by God with the ability to bring ideas to reality. Gerald Arbuckle – mentioned earlier in the context of lament – calls them 'dreamers who do'. The Church of England has in the past 20 years designated people who obviously have the charism of starting new things 'pioneers', following a translation of Hebrews 12.2, which encourages us to look to 'Jesus the pioneer and perfector of our faith'. At the Church Mission Society we use a variety of different terms for such people, including 'changemakers', 'fringe dwellers' and 'midwives of the new'.

The point is, such people are wired in a way that has significance for churches with a scarcity narrative because they can start stuff with little resources, make links across boundaries, network with people in other organizations and create teams. They can create possibility where there appeared to be none; sometimes over the medium to long term they can create new worshipping communities.

A skill we teach in Pioneering Parishes is how to identify people with this charism. Generally, they demonstrate most or all of the following characteristics: they have started stuff in the past – perhaps their own business or even something quite small, like a prayer group; they are resilient and resourceful and marked either by a passion for justice or a passion for sharing Jesus or both; they are good at gathering and connecting people from inside and outside the church and are often active members of the community; they are more comfortable with risks than the average person, more likely to have lived in a different culture, have skills of spiritual discernment and a responsiveness to the promptings of the Holy Spirit.

Owing to their gifts, skills and versatility, it is easy for people with this kind of profile to find a role – or even many roles – in sustaining church life, but they are usually happiest and most effectively deployed generating newness, and it is our conviction that God is calling creative entrepreneurial people into the church 'for such a time as this', and that they may form a part of God's strategic provision to help foster abundance in our churches at this time.

Pioneer types flourish best in environments of freedom and trust (obviously within safeguarding guidelines), so a light touch from oversight ministers and/or parish priests is called for as they step out. Once they begin to make links with other community groups, or churches of different denominations, boundaries may begin to blur and questions about ownership, returns on investment and assessing outcomes may arise. Perhaps in the context of abundance it is worth remembering here the adage that 'There is no limit to what we can achieve together if no one cares who gets the credit.' (For 'credit' here read 'fruit'.) Generosity between churches about which particular church grows, or which church adopts a new worshipping community as part of its ecosystem, is likely to help foster a generative and nurturing environment. When the primary objective of all churches is to offer spiritual care to a wider range of people in the whole neighbourhood, there will most likely be fewer hindrances to imaginative collaboration and a greater likelihood of seeing something beautiful emerge.

For congregational discussion

- *Who can we think of in the past tradition of the church that was called to 'start stuff'?*
- *Is there anyone in our current congregations who demonstrates many or all of the characteristics of a pioneer, change-maker, mission entrepreneur or 'midwife of the new'?*

With the hope in mind that new enterprises, worshipping communities and community groups may emerge from the work of a pioneering parish, we turn in the next chapter to the postures, practices, skills and tools for holding together a diversity of ways of being and doing church.

We finish this chapter with a summary of simple ways covered above of discovering and working with God's abundance in a pioneering parish (holding them together with the earlier dynamics of congregational spiritual discernment, a foundation of shared agreed principles, shifting the heart, attention and energy of the parish outwards):

- Acknowledge and lament loss.
- Teach the ecocycle and initiate conversations about seasons of life.
- Have the courage to take some activities through a process of 'creative destruction'.

- Identify and challenge prevailing scarcity narratives where necessary.
- Appreciate what you have and express gratitude.
- Value and celebrate volunteers.
- Encourage a fresh and evolving ecclesial imaginary.
- Ask: 'What do we have in our hand?'
- Hold and nurture space for new ideas.
- Identify, affirm and release dreamers who 'do'.
- Let go of questions of ownership, and give credit for what emerges.

5

Different Ways of Being and Doing Church: Equal, Connected and Distinct

We cultivate a range of different ways of being and doing church

We go to others because they are unlikely to come to us. In order to offer the cure of souls to a wider range of people, we look to see new expressions of church rising that are shaped in dialogue with the people they serve. We celebrate the equality of different forms of church, the new and the time-honoured together. We see ourselves as one part of a diverse range of credible, connected and distinctive forms of church, and rejoice in that diversity.

We go to others …

In Chapter 3 we explored 'Who is the church for?' Dietrich Bonhoeffer concluded: 'The church is only the church when it is the church for others.' So a dynamic mark of a pioneering parish is that we *go* – we go in Jesus' name with our hearts open, with an attentive disposition and our gifts, talents and energy at the service of the unconnected.

But why would we do this? Why would we not simply wait for others to come to us? Why would we be content with the approach suggested to me so many years ago in a parish that the 'villagers know where we are when they want us'?

We go to others because God in humility comes to us in Christ Jesus.

Within the Christian tradition, we go to others as the present embodiment of God in Christ who humbly set aside his place of privilege, status and power to draw alongside humanity. As Paul says in one of the oldest Christian hymns, 'who, though he was in the form of God, did not regard equality with God as something to be exploited, but emptied himself, taking the form of a slave' (Philippians 2.6–7). And again, 'though he was rich, yet for your sakes he became poor, so that by his poverty you might become rich' (2 Corinthians 8.9).

We go to others because God in humility seeks us out in Christ Jesus.

We are overwhelmed with joy when the Spirit of Jesus leads unconnected people to come to church. Yet one of my most unsettling realizations as a parish priest was that even when our parish church was 'doing church well' in terms of nurturing a credible space for the unconnected to come and explore and grow in the Christian faith, there were many, many more people who were unlikely to seek us out. We go to those who are unlikely to come to us because Jesus declared: 'As the Father sent me, so I send you' (John 20.21).

We go to others because we are sent by the humble God of Jesus who draws near to us.

Local Christian communities that authentically embody the humility of God in Christ recognize that the spiritual care of souls – traditionally known as the 'cure of souls' – extends far beyond any gathered congregation of believers. In the Anglican tradition especially, we go because we desire to expand the spiritual care of people within a wider community or network, to make tangible Christ's transforming love with greater effect and reach of engagement. By spiritual care, we do not exclusively limit this to proclamation (evangelism) or the observance of the occasional pastoral offices of baptisms, weddings and funerals. Spiritual care involves the whole person/community (please see the discussion in Chapter 1 on the Five Marks of Mission).

In a pioneering parish, the spiritual care of a local community is not the exclusive responsibility of the clergy (though pastors and priests in most denominations are given a public charge to fulfil this role). No – in a pioneering congregation the whole church shares in the privilege of offering spiritual care in Jesus' name.

We go to others because it embodies the spiritual care of a humble God who seeks all of us out.

For congregational reflection

- *Within our congregation, how comfortable are we with a 'go to' rather than 'come to us' approach?*
- *Who is responsible for spiritual care in our congregation? To what extent do we as a congregation recognize the privilege of offering spiritual care in Jesus' name to a whole community?*

Diverse forms of churches are needed to expand spiritual care

As we go out into all the parish in the humility of our God, we glimpse something of the great diversity within our communities – diversity that flows from our embodiment as humans, as well as life circumstances, interests and talents. Our encounter with variety is a challenge but also a fascinating one.

First, it is challenging because it reveals the untruth of certain narratives that we tell ourselves. For example, while serving as a priest in a team ministry of small villages outside Swindon, I often heard members of my various congregations say: 'Our parish church has something for everyone.' It was a lovely sentiment, but it was an illusion. Within the church building itself, public worship was always on Sunday and was largely a diet of 1662 Book of Common Prayer and Holy Communion. It was what the congregation members loved and wanted. What was on offer was not diverse in terms of day of the week and range of form.

Our encounter with diversity was also fascinating. As we drew alongside unconnected people in a relational way, we learned of people's life circumstances, joy and sadness, aspirations and talents. We discovered there was a hunger for God, but not what was on offer in the parish church. And through the sharing of life and dialogue, newness was unlocked and non-church members were willing to help us shape what church might look like.

Within our team ministry of four established congregations, new Christian communities alongside the parish churches emerged in a village hall, a scout hut and a local primary school. Each developing congregation had a unique expression and particular focus. Two of the fresh expressions of church were unapologetically children-focused. Diversifying how church was embodied naturally opened the opportunities to provide spiritual care for a wider range of unconnected people.

You might wonder how these fresh expressions fared over time. In this instance, two of our congregations did not last beyond two years; our third fresh expression of church celebrated its tenth birthday and is clearly no longer new.

People often ask whether diversifying through fresh expressions is worth it, especially when they are not designed to help build up the existing Sunday services or congregations. Frequently, the longer-standing forms of church worry about the sustainability of fresh expressions, fearful that they will become a financial burden. What a pioneering parish is concerned with is not sustainability but providing opportunities for spiritual care to a wider range of unconnected people. Often the emerging forms are for a season. Within its life span, however, it contributes to the offering of spiritual care to a wider range of unconnected people.

There is one significant caveat. All three fresh expressions mentioned above were worship service-centric. My best current understanding – based on years as a practitioner – is that the chances of sustainability can be increased when pioneer projects do not start with a worship service, but instead flow out of listening and loving service marked by missional humility.

As a new parish priest at St Mary's in Sholing, Southampton, I discovered that my predecessor had set me up to thrive as best he could. He took immensely difficult decisions long before I was on the scene. In particular, he oversaw the closure of a church building and congregation located on the Montague Avenue/Sullivan Road estate, which was an area of aspirational deprivation within the parish. The established model of church on this estate was simply unviable. The sad consequence following the closure of the church building and the moving of the congregation to the parish church was that there was little identifiable Christian presence in that area of the parish for a period of time.

Unexpectedly, the financial crisis of 2008 hit, and hit hard. Southampton City Council made a decision to close its youth services centres across the city, one of which was located on the Montague/Sullivan Road estate. Through the inspiration of our curate, Jon Oliver, and the support of the local civic councillors, the parish church arranged with the city to take responsibility for youth services within this area. In return, the PCC received possession of the small store-front youth services centre with peppercorn rates.

With a small group of volunteers from St Mary's and people of goodwill, a weekly youth club and homework club was offered. And this was the beginning of what emerged into Monty's Community Hub, a faith-based but not faith-biased community CIO (charitable incorporated organization). Monty's was set up as a CIO to ensure a long-term Christian commitment to the local community and ensure robust safeguarding and spiritual care, even if the Church of England at some point lost interest in the project. Our pioneers never hid the involvement of the church. But our missional humility – that willingness to listen to and serve in equal partnership with local residents, schools and community organizations – led to an increased sense of community spirit on this amazing estate.

Over the years many new, engaging activities emerged out of authentic relational dialogue with local residents, who felt a strong sense of ownership of Monty's Community Hub. All the great community work led to the funding of four part-time pioneer ministers, paid to do community work (not lead public acts of worship).

Through the present embodied humility of Jesus, our pioneers and volunteers were able to provide a depth of spiritual care for a wider range of unconnected people in a way that the traditional parish church model was unable to. Year after year our pioneers were accompanying/dwelling with local residents, helping them to know they were loved by God, exploring with them how to listen for God in Scripture and through service, all while embodying the humble presence of God in the community. Well over half a decade after the launch of Monty's Community Hub, Monty's Community Church emerged with its first act of public worship. Both the hub and church continue to this day as a credible, contextual, vibrant witness to the humble God who draws near in Jesus Christ.

For congregational reflection

- *What narratives/stories do we tell ourselves as a congregation that might be based on an illusion?*
- *How might unexpected circumstances provide us with an opportunity to do something different?*

Celebrating the new and time-honoured together

What the Monty's Community story illustrates is a celebration of new and time-honoured forms of church working together to extend spiritual care to a wider range of unconnected people. Monty's helps us to glimpse something of the emergence of a dynamic, diverse ecosystem.

The three sisters

The indigenous people of North America had a particular way of farming that sought to nurture a fruitful ecosystem of diversity. This has been described as the 'three sisters' model.

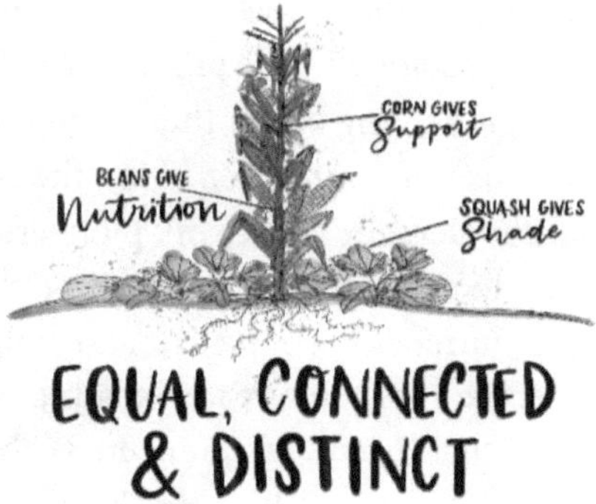

Figure 6: The three sisters model

Their practice involved the sowing of corn, beans and squash in a symbiotic relationship. The corn stalks provided a supportive framework for the growth of the beans. The bean shoots would climb the corn stalks while contributing nutrition to the soil by naturally depositing nitrogen. The squash leaves strengthened the vibrancy of the ecosystem by creating shade, which enabled the soil to remain moist. All three plants were equal in that they did what they naturally were designed to do. Through their connection with one another and the offering of a distinct contribution, a thriving environment for fruitfulness was possible.

In Pioneering Parishes we see the three sisters as a way of celebrating the equality, connectedness and distinctiveness of new and time-honoured forms of ministry.

Parochial ministry, in our analogy, is like the corn. Parish churches that are outward-looking and prioritize the engagement of unconnected people provide an energy and framework that supports new types of ministries both within the parish church and beyond.

Pioneer ministers – both lay and ordained – are like the beans. In a thriving ecology where pioneers are supported by a parish church's pioneering ethos, there is missional energy flowing from a sense of connection. Like the beans, which give nutritional supplement to the soil, pioneers make a distinct contribution to the missional ecology and the parochial. Typically, parish churches expect this contribution to be an influx of new people into the already existing services, failing to understand that the role of pioneers is about forming new, contextual congregations. Perhaps the unique contribution that pioneers make to parish congregations is to remind long-standing members, and model for them, the pioneering nature of the church.

There is another dynamic within the ecosystem. Within congregations there are a group of people who advocate for and enable pioneers. These advocates are like the squash plants, which provide shade and protection. The role of a pioneer advocate is to make the environment conducive for fruitfulness within a diverse ecosystem that celebrates the new and time-honoured together. We shall explore the place of advocacy in a diverse missional ecology in the next section.

Pioneering parishes are marked by celebration of equality, connectedness and diversity. Such parishes hold a variety of expressions of church together, recognizing that many forms of church are needed to engage appropriately with a wider range of unconnected people.

For congregational reflection

- *What examples of new and time-honoured expressions of church do we have in our parish?*

- *How is a sense of equality, connection and distinctiveness expressed between them? What might be done to develop the strength of the diverse church ecosystem in our area/parish/congregation?*

Pioneer advocacy within a diverse church ecology

Pioneer advocates, says Dave Male, the former co-director of Vision and Strategy for the Church of England and author of *How to Pioneer (even if you haven't a clue)*,[1] are 'key people for the future of the church'. Advocates, as in the three sisters analogy, nurture and negotiate space for a thriving missional ecology.

In his book *Refounding the Church*, Gerald Arbuckle spoke about the characteristics of pioneer advocacy.[2] Although he used the language of 'authority dissenter', Arbuckle was describing what we call 'pioneer advocacy'. Basically, pioneer advocates are 'insiders' who dwell within time-honoured forms of church but who recognize the need for a thriving mixed ecology of church. They are deeply committed and loyal to the local church but are dissatisfied with congregational cultures that give priority to those who are already connected. Frequently, advocates are people who have some influence to help shape discussions and decision-making. They may be members of PCCs, elders, deacons, licensed lay ministers, associate pastors/priests or vicars/senior pastors.

1 David Male, 2016, *How to Pioneer (even if you haven't a clue)*, London: Church House Publishing.

2 Gerald Arbuckle, 1993, *Refounding the Church: Dissent for Leadership*, London: Geoffrey Chapman.

Pioneer advocates are characterized by their embodiment of a mixed ecology posture. Posture here, metaphorically speaking, is about outlook and an attitude that influences actions. Initially, as I personally was growing into the role, I thought of pioneer advocacy in terms of strategies and techniques to be mastered. I quickly realized that this role is far more about posture and embodiment.

What does this posture look like in a mixed ecology? Pioneer advocacy essentially is the embodiment of all the five dynamics explored in this book. In relation to celebrating the new and time-honoured together, it involves two postures: nurturing partnership and guiding.

Advocates as nurturers of partnership between diverse forms of church

Pioneer advocates nurture connection between diverse forms of church. In my personal experience, the initial (and unspoken) expectation of existing congregations has been that pioneers (people serving in emerging forms of church) are responsible for maintaining and managing the relationship.

There is, however, a growing awareness that the advocates are the most appropriate people to initiate the bridging work, for they understand the structures of the time-honoured church while also appreciating the need for the entrepreneurial spirit of the pioneers.

Pioneering Parishes takes seriously the need to grow partnerships within the mixed ecology of new and time-honoured. The time-honoured model of church has the primary responsibility for cultivating good relationships with pioneers. In my role as Pioneer Development Officer in the Diocese of Portsmouth I crafted six top tips for pioneers to enable them to build constructive relationships with their incumbent colleagues. In response to the top tips for pioneers, Tina recently crafted six top tips for parish clergy and congregations (which mirrored the originals to a certain extent), to nurture partnership with those serving in new forms of church. They are:

- *Take time to get to know your pioneer as a human being.* Whatever you've heard about pioneers or pioneering, you haven't met this pioneer before. Try to understand why this particular pioneer is on this particular pathway.
- *Trust your pioneer.* Pioneers need to be trusted. They will flourish and be fruitful if they are given space to explore, experiment and fail in an atmosphere of trust. Be willing to take risks with them and support them to do courageous things.
- *Champion your pioneer.* Become your pioneer's greatest advocate. Explain what the pioneer is trying to do with anyone who will listen. Do it with the same level of passion and simplicity as you would when talking to someone who knows little about Jesus.
- *Model equality of relationship.* All forms of church are church. They are all equal to one another, connected with one another and distinct from one another. Model this equality, connection and distinctiveness in your relationship with your pioneer. Be generous and humble in respect to your fellow leader, however slowly their congregation is developing or however much excitement and energy is being created by something new.
- *Think win–win.* Parish priests and pioneers can easily become takers. Thinking win–win means finding ways to strategically support one another. Explore ways you might

invest in your pioneer's ministry, and seek to exceed your pioneer's expectations.

- *Aspire to be your best.* What kind of person do you aspire to be for God? Aspire to be a better person each day. Practise generosity, vulnerability, patience and courtesy – and show goodwill.

Our experience is that pioneers deeply value authentic, uncontrolling relationships with parish churches. Often this is an essential ingredient for fruitfulness within both new and time-honoured forms of church.

Advocates as guides on the pioneering journey

Advocates are guides who intentionally take congregations on a pioneering journey because we cannot see what God has to show us from where we are at present. This usually involves taking parish churches into a pilgrimage through the unknown in search of what God wants to reveal. The journey into the unfamiliar aspires to discover a new understanding of what it means to embody God's humility within a diverse ecology of church.

Insight and learning require both time and grace. In Pioneering Parishes training sessions, I have noticed that the 'three sisters' approach to diversity has generally proved theoretically acceptable. Yet what is not initially apparent is that within an emerging diversity, everything in the ecosystem has to adjust the way it relates to other distinctive forms. In an ecosystem of equality, connection and distinctiveness, a new dynamic way of existing is required in order to thrive. It requires that each form of church moves from seeing itself as the centre of importance to a position of mutuality and connection.

This is a challenging shift because each distinct form of church – whether it is emerging or has been around for a long time – tends to operate with itself at the centre and expects other forms to revolve around what is happening within 'our' form of ministry. At every stage of church life, this is a reality. And it is not just the long-standing existing forms of church that fall into this way of being and operating, though they are often the primary perpetrators of such attitudes and behaviour. Pioneer advocates, pioneers and new expressions of church are also susceptible to placing themselves 'at the centre', forgetting that the aspiration of a pioneering congregation is a diverse ecology that enables the whole church to engage a wider range of unconnected people within a community.

The equality of connection is the opposite of operating as though we were the centre. What I think equality looks like is when each form of Christian community takes itself out of the centre, no longer seeing itself as the most important, strongest and essential part, and starts operating with a disposition of missional humility within a diverse ecology of church.

'Let the same mind be in you that was in Christ Jesus, who, though he was in the form of God, did not regard equality with God as something to be exploited' (Philippians 2.5–6). What Paul is driving at in quoting from the oldest Christian hymn is that the demonstration of equality is engaging meaningfully in relationship with the other, not seeking to advantage ourselves by operating from a position or place of superiority and power.

For the existing congregations, equality is demonstrated in our willingness to give up control in an attempt to shore up our own lack and future.

'Those "churches" which would save themselves,' says Jesus, 'will lose themselves.'

Preoccupation with ourselves – often expressed in our frantic efforts to preserve what we love by drawing resources, talents and energy to ourselves – is to behave as though we are at the centre of it all. Equality is expressed in prioritizing connection and moving in our thoughts and actions towards the margins of church to where unconnected people are.

Of course, with the prioritizing of a diverse ecology of church, a significant tension within the parish church often emerges. Often, long-standing members of existing congregations begin to sense a shift in emphasis. The amount of attention they once received is no longer as ample. They might begin to say: 'We're not important any more. Only new people, younger people, unconnected people are valued.'

What is happening in such instances is a well-recognized occurrence within a change process. There is a saying, adapted here, that rings true: 'When you're accustomed to privilege, equality feels like oppression.' When you're used to all the attention and having things done your way and for you, sharing with others is difficult.

This is where pioneer advocates need both courage and sensitivity when helping long-standing members of existing congregations to navigate the journey towards an equal, connected and distinct ecology of church. Shifting to operate in a more pioneer way does require adjustments. Some treasured things will be lost. Yet this is an essential part of the journey, not to be avoided. It is the responsibility and privilege of pioneer advocates to help people navigate the change they are experiencing.

At this point I could offer techniques for accomplishing this. One of my significant realizations as a pioneer advocate was that the most challenging encounters on the pioneering parishes journey were not with the unconnected people in our community. Nor were the most taxing conversations with the people in our congregations who struggled to adapt to the implications of a mixed-ecology ethos. The most difficult encounters were always with myself. I learned that being a pioneer advocate within a pioneering congregation required me to be more than a good leader. The task of leadership calls me to be a better human being.

Along the pioneering journey towards a diverse ecology of church, leaders – both lay and ordained – will come face to face with significant dynamics that require undertaking deep inner work. The pioneering adventure involves nurturing a well-kept heart with Jesus, our humble and generous Pioneer.

There are many narratives that will confront leaders along the way. Within the transition towards a diverse ecology of church, some of the most dramatic voices congregational leaders will encounter are:

- 'I'm not needed anymore' (feeling redundant);
- 'What do you think you're doing?' (serving under intense criticism);
- 'I know what I'm doing!' (pride);
- 'It's all a house of cards!' (instability).

'I'm not needed any more' (feeling redundant)

In the time-honoured model, the parish church is pictured in the centre at the heart of a community. Where does the time-honoured fit into all those ambitious visions for the future? Why does the church press for – and diocesan communications almost exclusively celebrate – new forms of ministry? How can the parish clergy simply be dismissed as 'limiting factors'? Why should such effort and care be expended when the parish church is no longer valued?

Frequently these are the questions that clergy ask. Sometimes lay leadership in local congregations may intuit these same questions as they observe the changing landscape within their denomination. What is all the more challenging is that these types of questions do not go away when congregational leaders have embarked on the unpaved path of the pioneering journey. In some cases, feelings are amplified when off grid.

Pioneering Parishes strongly affirms the role of the local congregation/parish church in providing spiritual care within a geographical place or network. The surprising discovery is that as clergy and congregations journey along the pioneering path, a renewed sense of vocation can emerge. Key to this reworked expression of vocation is the realization that faithfulness often requires the church to see and do things differently. And in venturing along the pilgrimage of greater connection, clergy and parish churches begin to glimpse that they are far from redundant. Rather, there is still a significant contribution to make in connecting with the unconnected in our parishes.

'What do you think you're doing?' (serving under intense criticism)

When embarking on, and persevering with, a pioneering journey, it soon becomes clear that this quickly exposes 'the elephant within congregations': the need for change in the way we understand and do things. With each step of adjustment and relinquishment, leaders discover that everyone has an opinion about what is happening. It can quickly leave leaders – both lay and ordained – feeling as if they are doing something wrong in questioning what is in existence and seeking alternative approaches within the congregation. I once had a member of the congregation, an owner of a successful local business, write me several long letters objecting to how I allocated the use of my staff team's assignments.

What is often most unexpected for many clergy in particular is the discovery that some of the most challenging criticism can come from colleagues. For instance, in what was supposed to be a safe space for vicars to reflect on their supervision of clergy colleagues, I shared how I was collaborating with my pioneers. My approach was met with immediate hostility in the group. Why aren't you expecting pioneers to support you in occasional offices? Why aren't your pioneers saying daily prayer with you? How can you let those pioneers get away with not doing things within the parish church? On another occasion, at the ordination of my pioneer curate, a priest berated me as we walked in procession down the centre aisle of the cathedral for not making my colleague conform to the expectations of what clergy looked/sounded like.

There is much talk within the church of faithfulness. Careful listening to this narrative sometimes reveals that what people mean is 'Don't tamper or change the way things are done.' Yet faithfulness to God sometimes means that we have to do things differently.

Stepping off the well-worn paved path of expectations and ways of doing things within a congregation requires courageous honesty. As much as one wrestles with the desire to step back on to the well-trodden path, those leading in pioneering congregations will have a nagging sense that to do so is unwise. Courageous honesty, in this instance, flows from the unshakeable realization that even when a parish church is functioning in an attractive way, many will never come to us as we are. The cure (or care) of souls bids us to diversify what we're doing in order that we may actually attempt to go into all the parish.

'I know what I'm doing!' (pride)

There is a real tension between being knowledgeable and knowing what you're doing. Over the years, being 'lectured' by parishioners who assume that I know nothing about managing change has been a source of deep irritation. I've often had the following run through my mind: 'I'm not an amateur; I know what I am doing.' There is a sense in which this may be accurate. Equally, this potentially is also a flag for lurking pride.

One may have a degree of confidence about the need to step off the path. This, however, is not the same thing as knowing what you're doing. With that single decision, leaders and congregations quickly discover that the nature of the journey changes from some certainty to ongoing experimentation. Often this way of embodying life in the parish church means extra attention needs to be given to listening deeply.

There will be those who don't think the leaders know what they are doing. The tendency is for leaders to distance themselves from those who see/think differently. The humble action of listening carefully to those who have a different perspective – and may even want to get back on to the paved path – can potentially unlock insight. Sometimes the very people who disagree with us contribute the insights needed to take the next step forward on the unpaved path.

'It's all a house of cards!' (instability)

Within a pioneering parish there is often the feeling that what is being built is 'all a house of cards'. We are programmed to expect stability within firm and solid structures. Church leaders can easily fret about holding together the time-honoured and the emerging, almost feeling like failures for being unable to stabilize what is now fragile.

Congregations are rarely prepared for fragility and instability. Nor are these things desired. Yet in the midst of all the uncertainty and change swirling around us, there is a deep unlocking within those leaders who recognize 'it's all a house of cards' as a new reality in church life emerges.

In such an environment, leaders of pioneering parishes quickly come to the end of their own resources. It brings whole leadership teams into a liminal space of engaging in the deep spiritual work of relinquishing the aspiration for success, powerful results and reputation. The fragility of the situation confronts leaders to sit with the uncomfortable perceptions that the pioneering parishes experiment looks a lot like failure much of the time.

And here the Benedictine monastic tradition has much to teach pioneering parishes. At the heart of the Benedictine way of life is the commitment to inner stability – the vocation to stay put when we can only think of walking away, keeping one's eyes fixed on the task set before us, and recognizing that in such situations God has much to show us about ourselves for the benefit of many others.

The mixed ecology of church is not for the faint-hearted

Participating in the journey of pioneering congregation is not for the faint-hearted. The call to such a challenge demands much of us, perhaps more than we've ever been led to believe. In truth, embodying this diverse way of being church requires a commitment to the generosity of Jesus, *the* Pioneer. In this, we join the transforming adventure of 'reaching beyond the current stretch of the church' in Jesus' name.

Conclusion

If you have got to this point in the book, you will have understood that, as we see it, the Church of England is – just like Abraham and Sarah and numerous other characters of the Bible and the tradition before them – on a journey with God to a new place.

We are persuaded that the work of parish priests today is not to try to restore the parish church to its former state (whatever that may have been), or to try to set a vision for the future and organize all our energies and resources towards attaining this goal (although a vision may arise in the process of becoming a pioneering parish). We believe we are being called into a state of uncertainty, fragility and adventure, in pursuit of what the Partnership for Missional Church team (see Chapter 1) would call 'God's preferred and promised future', which can only be discerned through an ongoing practice of attention to where God is leading.[1]

The practices for congregational spiritual discernment are vital for enabling the people of God to be present to the realities of the moment, both inside and outside the church. The tools described in Chapter 2, along with most of the other tools we offer, create conditions for honest and open

1 Nigel Rooms, 2025, 'Being Witness at the End of Modernity: Paradigm Shifts in Mission for the English Parish Church', in Paul Bradbury, Isabelle Hamley and Andy Smith (eds), *Being the People of God: Missional Ecclesiology for Uncertain Times*, London: SCM Press, pp. 112–24.

conversations about what is true in the life of the congregation, and what is observably considered to be true by ordinary people about life within the geographical boundaries of the parish. With this data available from many sources being brought into worship services and church meetings (all congregation members being empowered through the participatory tools to share their noticings), we are better able to sift and find patterns in what is coming to light. Then we can prayerfully discern the path or paths through all the possible courses of action – or inaction – that God the Holy Spirit is inviting us to follow.

Setting values in place, allowing principles rather than personal preferences to consistently shape attitudes, behaviour and decision-making establishes a firm foundation for participatory change. Values given specific three-dimensional character through evidence descriptors act as a tool for congregational formation, providing embodied exemplars of what it looks like when we inhabit familiar Christian virtues. Regular evaluation of progress towards the values embeds practices and processes through which everyone, clergy included, may aspire together towards a more Christlike nature, collectively and individually.

We are convinced that a values-based foundation reduces the breadth and scale of conflict in situations of congregation culture change. Conflict still arises, but the values set the boundaries on what questions are up for debate, and which have been definitively settled as expressed in the agreed missional written values statements.

The tools, postures, practices and skills we offer aim at increasing connection. In church – as in society – we are impoverished by a lack of deep connection with others. In Pioneering Parishes we are convinced that the Holy Spirit is calling us all to move courageously towards those we don't know, understand or who we may even fear, and to invest in real relationships and develop systems for open and transparent decision-making that include little-heard voices as well as more privileged ones. The desire for deepening connection, the exchange of gifts with others and the inclusion of all apply equally to our engagement with others in the church, and those in the community with whom we long to share the love of God in Christ so we might all in time grow into fullness of life in him.

We have tried to show how the incarnation of God in Christ provides the rationale and impetus for this kind of radical outward-and-downward movement of the church towards its community in a posture of self-giving love. We have also offered practical tools to support this process in Sargeant's matrix, the ecocycle, other tools for congregational spiritual discernment, and the decision-making matrix, along with a few stories of our own ministries and of people we have personally journeyed with – and learned from – to provide practical examples of how the Pioneering Parishes approach can bring fruit.

Clearly, we need to approach these times when resources can be scarce with a fresh imagination of what church may look like and a deep trust that even when it feels hopeless and we wonder if God has deserted us, a time will come when there are surprising springs in the desert. It will require qualities of resilience and adaptability, skills of improvisation and a willingness to accept that it may at times feel as if we are trying to stop a house of cards from collapsing into nothing. Acts of lament are an apt compassionate pastoral response to support a congregation moving into a new season, or as a way of responding to failure; they may also reduce the levels of anger and frustration directed at the instigators of change, and bring deeper causes of resistance to light.

Always the key aim of a pioneering parish is to offer spiritual care to a wider range of people, particularly those who are unconnected. This kind of care may be encompassed by any of the Five Marks of Mission: it may meet practical, emotional, financial or physical needs; it may transform unjust social structures that disadvantage and marginalize; it may be care for the planet that provides for our very existence; it may be the opening of a door into the presence of Christ or a demonstration of what it means to be a follower of Jesus through an attractive life lived for God and others; it may mean inviting people to church or explaining the gospel story; it will be varied, and open to the incomparably sensitive and appropriate interventions of the Holy Spirit.

As we've been writing the final chapters of the book we have been very encouraged to read the results of recent research into the effectiveness of our training through webinar series and, increasingly, in face-to-face training for dioceses, deaneries and occasionally individual PCCs. We hear of churches that are coming alive with excitement as they move outwards into their communities and find new possibilities of connection, capacity and collaboration. Church leaders who have done Pioneering Parishes training describe how they have taken from the tools what has been useful. Often it is the fresh imagination of what it might mean to 'be church' that animates their congregations. Critical to this kind of ministry is the skill of pioneer advocacy and the demanding inner spiritual work this requires if a thriving mixed ecology of church is to emerge by God's grace over time.

Throughout the book we have tried to put at the centre the model of Christ portrayed by the apostle Paul in Philippians 2: venturing to earth and taking on human flesh in indescribable humility. Pioneering Parishes attempts to flag this humility as the core value of the mixed ecology, and a necessary condition for a church ecosystem to develop, grow and thrive. Unless each and every one of us, wherever we find ourselves in this system of church, is willing to accept the need to work with the Spirit of God through prayer and practice to remove ourselves from the centre, prioritize connection over power and acknowledge the equality of all individuals and churches with in it, we will make limited progress.

We adopted the image of the three sisters – the corn, squash and beans growing together in mutual gift exchange – three years after our training enterprise began, and we found the words 'equal, connected and distinct' to go with the picture. Greg and I are persuaded that these three words are sufficient to describe the network of interdependent relationships that characterize the body of Christ at a human individual level and at church level too. When we understand we are all uniquely ourselves (distinct), connected (in relationship with God, others and ourselves) and equal (created equal with all others in God's image for God's glory), we have an imaginary of how all the parts of a newly emerging way of being and doing church can flow together as we make fledgling attempts to move out towards those who do not yet belong and have much to teach us still.

It is not an easy journey to undertake and, as we said at the beginning, there is no map or blueprint; there are no straightforward answers and no guarantee of new or larger churches at the end of it. But if you are ready to step out (or are well on the way and are here looking for fresh input), we believe God will meet you in the aspiration to be caught up in the flow of the Holy Spirit and carry you (admittedly on bumpy air currents) into the coming future. Our prayers go with you.

Further Reading

Arbuckle, Gerald, 1993, *Refounding the Church: Dissent for Leadership*, London: Geoffrey Chapman.

Bradbury, Paul, 2024, *In the Fullness of Time: A Story From the Past and Future of the Church*, Norwich: Canterbury Press.

Cray, Graham, 2024, *On Mission with Jesus: Changing the Default Setting of the Church*, Norwich: Canterbury Press.

Sparks, Paul, Tim Soerens and Dwight J. Friesen, 2014, *The New Parish: How Neighborhood Churches are Transforming Mission, Discipleship and Community*, Downers Grove, IL: InterVarsity Press.

Strohm, Deacon Keith, 2019, *Ablaze: 5 Essential Paradigm Shifts for Parish Renewal*, Frederick, MD: Word Among Us Press.

www.ingramcontent.com/pod-product-compliance
Lightning Source LLC
Chambersburg PA
CBHW050226220826
50226CB00037B/537
* 9 7 8 1 7 8 1 4 0 4 7 6 8 *